MW01089877

How to Dye Your Own Fabric

An introduction to dyeing fabrics at home including **5 projects** for you to try

Margo Price

Publishing and Legal Notices

Copyright

Copyright © 2015 Margo Price. All rights reserved.

This publication may not, in whole or in part, be reproduced, transmitted, transcribed, stored in a retrieval system, or translated in any form or by any means without prior written consent of Margo Price.

Liability

We have used our best efforts to ensure that the content of this document is both useful and correct at the time of publication. The content of this document is supplied for information only and is subject to change without notice. The authors assume no responsibility or liability for any errors or inaccuracies that may appear in this document, nor the use to which it may be put.

This document is for information only and does not represent a legal contract or agreement.

Publishing Information

Author: Margo Price
                     www.time4me-
                     workshops.co.uk

Editor/Designer: Andrew A Moore

Published By: AAM Design Limited
                     www.aamdesign.co.uk

Publication Number: T4M-004

Issue Number: 2

Issue Date: October 2015

About this Document

This document is based on the dyeing methods and used by Margo Price while running Time4me Workshops. This document describes how to prepare and dye cellulose or plant based fabrics using Procion MX Fibre-reactive dyes.

Contents

Part 1: Introduction to Dyeing

Why on earth would anyone want to dye their own fabrics?

 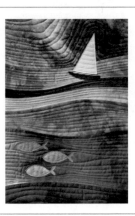  

Welcome

If you are reading this book, you have probably never asked yourself the question: "Why on earth would anyone want to dye their own fabrics?". In these pages I will show how simple it is to create a whole new world of colour that will inspire you to create unique stitched and embroidered projects.

Why Do I Dye?

I have been teaching machine sewing for over twelve years and have been dyeing my own fabrics for most of that time, both for my students and for my own creations.

My nearest, decent, fabric shop is an hour's train ride away. They sell a wide selection of plain and printed fabrics in most of the well-known ranges, but often I cannot find exactly what I want. This is no reflection on the shop, but since I have discovered fabric dyeing, shop-bought fabrics seem pale and uninteresting. They just cannot deliver the zing that my home-produced, procion-dyed fabrics can.

The variety and intensity of the coloured fabrics you can produce are entirely under your control. By following my colour recipes, you too will be able to create any colour you require to help you with your sewing or other craft projects.

A Whole New World of Colour

When you visit a fabric shop, or even buy on-line, your choice is limited to whatever is on offer. But once you get the hang of dyeing, you can create whatever colour you want and even a good many that you didn't want – at first…

One of the most exciting things about dyeing is the element of surprise. When you're not in need of any particular colour and you just allow yourself to experiment, you will be amazed at what you can come up with. Some pieces you may not like at all, but you can change them. If you're using a good quality fabric – and we'll get to that in a minute – you can overdye any that are not quite your thing, until they're just right.

A Safe and Easy Process

Dyeing is not difficult. There are chemicals involved, and a fair amount of mess, but with a bit of care and attention to detail, home dyeing is easily achievable by almost anyone. Very little specialist equipment is required and you probably have most of the general equipment already. Anything you don't have can usually be picked up cheaply at a supermarket or discount store.

Economy

Commercially-dyed and printed fabrics are expensive and, as long as labour prices in the Far East continue to rise, the price will keep on rising. High quality mercerized cotton fabric, ready prepared for dyeing and printing (PFD), if you buy it in lengths of at least 10 yards (or metres), can work out at less than half the price, per metre, than commercial fabrics. And it is usually 60" wide; instead of the traditional 45" width of those you buy.

I buy my dyeing fabric, in 60m bolts, from a former mill town in the North of England. I am not under any misapprehension that it is woven there any longer, but it is heartening to be able to buy it in the same country!

Initial outlay for dyes and chemicals, can be quite expensive, but you need only three basic primary colours to begin with, and black. I say begin with, but I have been dyeing for over five years now and still only buy basic primaries and black. I may buy a different shade of primary occasionally to mix things up a bit, but I still prefer to experiment with mixing my own colours rather than buy ready-mixed.

If you find this book useful and inspiring please leave me a review at www.Amazon.com or www.Amazon.co.uk and let me know, either through my website, www.time4me-workshops.co.uk, or my facebook page www.facebook.com/pages/Margo-Price-Author . Similarly, if you have any questions or problems then I'd like to hear about that too.

Margo Price

The dyes are very economical and a little goes a long way, as you will find when you start to clean up after a dye session.

All the other equipment you will need is cheap and readily available, if indeed, you don't have it already.

What's In This Book?

This book will provide you with the information you need to feel confident about dyeing fabrics in your own home.

Part 1: Introduction to Dyeing

Part 1 will help you to answer such questions as:

- Which fabrics can I dye?
- Which dyes and chemicals will I need?
- What equipment will I need?

Part 2: The Dyeing Process

Part 2 takes you step-by-step through the dyeing process, and the importance of keeping records of your dyeing projects.

- **Stage 1** - Preparing your fabrics for dyeing.
- **Stage 2** - Mixing your dyes.
- **Stage 3** - Setting up your equipment.
- **Stage 4** - Immersing your fabric in the dye.
- **Stage 5** - Finishing off by rinsing, scouring, trimming and ironing your dyed fabric.

Part 3: Dyeing a 12-Step Colour Wheel

Part 3 provides an overview of colour theory and introduces you to the basic colour wheel and how to reproduce all these colours from primary colour dyes.

Part 4: Getting More From Your Colour Wheels

Part 4 explains how to go beyond the basic colour wheel and produce intermediate steps, alternative colours and muted tones.

Part 5: Projects to Dye For

Part 5 provides a variety of colourful projects that you may wish to tackle in order to reinforce your new-found dyeing skills and add to your knowledge of colour.

Part 6: Further Reading

Part 6 describes other related books and websites where you can find more inspiration and advice to help you become more skilful with your sewing machine.

Fabrics for Dyeing

The success or failure of any dyeing project depends largely on the fabric you choose. Fabrics come in a huge range of weights, constructions and compositions and it is very important to choose one which will give the best possible results for your project. Not only will this prevent you having to go back and repeat the whole process again but it will be a huge boost to your confidence in your ability to dye your own fabrics.

Fabric Construction

First, let's talk a little about how fabrics are constructed and why some are suitable for dyeing and some aren't.

Fabric generally falls into three types: woven. non-woven and knit.

Woven Fabrics

Woven fabric is the most commonly used for home dyeing. It is formed from two sets of threads, the *warp*, which runs lengthwise, and the *weft*, which runs widthways. Woven fabrics are available in simple or complex weaves. Simple weaves can be muslin, denim and some types of sheeting while complex weaves can be corduroy or towelling.

Woven Fabric

Non-Woven Fabrics

Non-woven fabric is generally defined as a set of threads or filaments which are entangled, by some mechanical means, and then bonded thermally or chemically. They are commonly made with by-products from the plastics and oil and petrochemical industries and are used for making very specific products. These can include single use, bacteria-resistant products for hospitals and schools, tea-bags and packaging. Non-woven fabric can be made with some recycled materials and does not require the raw materials to be turned into yarn before construction, so it considered to be quite ecologically friendly – but not great for dyeing.

Non-woven Fabric

Knit Fabrics

Knit fabrics can be divided into two types, warp knits such as tricot, which are generally used for t-shirts, and weft knits, which are generally hand or machine-knitted. The main difference between the two is that weft knits unravel when cut but warp knits, while they may fray a little, don't unravel.

Hand-knitted Weft Products

Fabric Composition

Fabric can be made of natural fibres or man-made (synthetic).

Natural Fabrics

Natural fibres can be divided into two groups: cellulose and protein.

Cellulose-based fabrics are made from plant fibres and protein fabrics from animal-based fibres. Examples of cellulose fabrics are linen jute, cotton, rayon. Viscose and rayon, although subject to some chemical engineering, are made of wood and can be classified as 'natural'.

Protein fibres can be wool, silk, alpaca, angora, mohair and feathers.

Synthetic Fabrics

As the technology of chemical engineering increases, so does the range of man-made fibres. Man-made, or synthetic fibres, are the result of scientific research to improve on naturally occurring fibres. Natural fibres, whether plant or animal, all have their own peculiarities. Filaments are different lengths and thicknesses and don't all lay in the same direction which can cause problems in their commercial use.

Today, the synthetic fabric which dominates our clothing industry is made from synthesised polymers which are melted and drawn into long threads. The raw materials which these fibres are made from, and the regularity of their size, make them ideal for use in mass production.

As you can probably tell, I find the manufacture of fibre and cloth an endlessly fascinating subject – but back to dyeing…

Fabrics Suitable for Dyeing

The Procion MX Fibre-reactive dyes, which I use in my home-dyeing projects, are designed for use with cellulose fibres. Silk, although technically a protein fibre (as it is obtained from the larvae of a silkworm), can also be dyed successfully with Procion dyes.

Other protein fibres require acid-based dyes and heating for successful colouring. These are outside the scope of this book but will be covered in detail in a further planned book on yarn dyeing.

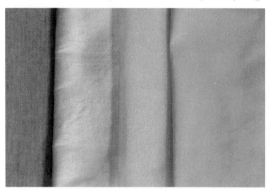

Cellulose Fibres Suitable for Dyeing - from Left to Right, Loose-weave Muslin, Slubbed Silk, Silk Organza, Tight-weave, Mercerized PFD Cotton.

PFD Cottons

In this book, the dyeing projects will mostly be described using a tightly-woven, mercerized and bleached 100% cotton fabric. The *mercerizing* process aids dye absorption resulting in a greater depth of colour, while bleaching, as it removes any background colour, results in brighter finish to the dyed piece. This fabric is widely available from manufacturers which supply materials to textile artist and small clothing producers. It can be obtained as PFD (Prepared for Dyeing and Printing) which means any sizing or starch has been removed. This has the advantage that you don't need to wash it before dyeing.

Fabrics from the High Street

Naturally, if this is your first attempt at dyeing your own fabrics, you will probably want to do a little experimenting with smaller pieces of fabric before you have great bolts of the stuff delivered to your front door.

Be aware that any cotton fabrics, which you buy from fabric shops or department stores, unless marked otherwise, have probably been treated with *sizing*. This improves the appearance and handling of the fabric while on the bolt but does make it resistant to dyeing. If you decide to use these fabrics, you will need to wash them thoroughly before attempting to dye them. Specialist scouring agents are available for this and these are described in the next section.

How to Tell What Your Fabric is Made of

Fabric, particularly if you are buying it in one of the discount fabric shops, is commonly mis-labelled. Many of these shops source their fabrics from the Far East and are unsure what they're getting. When you are buying fabric for dyeing, you need to be 100% sure that the fabric you are buying is **100% natural fibre** or your trip, and your money, will have been wasted.

Most fabric shops will be willing to give you a small sample swatch of a fabric you are interested in and, by carrying out a few simple tests, you can be sure that you are getting what you need.

The Bleach Test

Pour a small amount of household bleach in to a bowl and dip the corner of your fabric into it. If the colour discharges, and you are left with a white or pale area, the fabric is a natural fibre.

The Burn Test

Place your fabric on a ceramic or glass plate and light the corner with a match. If it burns to a friable ash with the smell of burning hair, then it is a natural fibre. If it burns to a hard bead, it is

synthetic and cannot be dyed using the processes described in this book.

Dyes and Chemicals

In this section I will tell you about the essential supplies you will need for a colourful result. With just three primary colours – red yellow and blue (and black) you can make a whole range of beautiful hues.

Safety First

All the dyes and chemicals used in this book are generally considered to be non-toxic. You should, however, take precautions during their use:

- Never inhale or swallow the dyes or chemicals, and never eat, smoke or drink while using them – as these activities can increase the risk of ingestion of airborne particles.

- Always work in an area that is well-ventilated – but not breezy as this can cause particles to become airborne.

- While handling dyes in dry-powder form, always wear a mask that is approved for working with fine-particle dust. Close the container immediately after measuring out the required amount of dye powder. Avoid all actions that may cause the particles to become airborne and take particular care if you wear contact lenses.

- When handling dye in powder and solution, wear rubber gloves. The dye will stain and can take a few days to wash off.

- Keep a separate set of utensils, vessels and containers for dyeing sessions and never use them for food.

- Ensure that all chemicals and dyes are labelled and stored safely, in their original containers if at all possible. Store them out of reach of children and pets.

- If you are pregnant or breast-feeding avoid contact with dyes and chemicals.

Dyes - Primary Colours

Procion MX fibre reactive dyes are synthetic dyes that are intended for use with natural plant-based or cellulose fibres. They are easy to use, easy to mix and provided a range of light-fast, clear bright colours. They are available from suppliers around the world and come in a range of great colours.

The best thing about them though, in my opinion, is that with just three primary colours – red yellow and blue (plus black!) you can make a whole range of beautiful shades. Of course, these primaries also come in various forms. Those that are not mixed with other colours will produce the purest shades.

Red can be Cerise, Intense Red, Scarlet and Magenta

Blue can be Royal, Navy, Cobalt and Cerulean

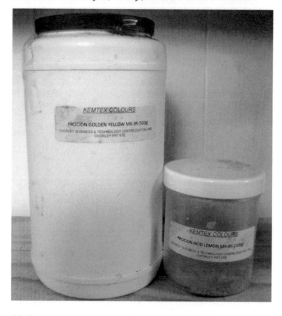

Yellow can be Acid, Golden and Marigold.

So by just sticking to these three primaries, in their particular variations, you will never run out of new combinations to discover.

Varying Primary Colours

Understanding Procion MX Dyes

When you go to your dye supplier to purchase your first selection of dyes, you will be faced with a dizzying array of letters and numbers which signify the properties of each dye.

Example:

"PROCION INDIGO NAVY MX-2G (500g)"

Each dye name usually comprises:

- The **brand name** - "Procion" for example.
- A **colour name** - Golden Yellow, Cerulean Blue, etc.
- A **prefix** - which signifies the type of dye – "MX" stands for Dichloritriazine. Always ask for this.
- An **optional number** - indicates how much more of a colour is in a dye. For example 8B is bluer than 5B. This is followed by letter, usually, G, R or B, which signify the following German colour names:
  - **Gelb** = Yellow (note this is not Green)
  - **Rot** = Red
  - **Blau** = Blue
- The **weight** - "500g" a big tub, "100g" a small tub, etc.

Sometimes a dye may just have a letter after the dash rather than a number and a letter. Examples of these are Blue MX-R, which, by virtue of the red component, may have a purplish cast and Blue MX-G which, by virtue of the yellow may appear slightly green.

Yellow MX8G	Yellow MX4G	Yellow MX4RA	Yellow MX2RA	Orange MX2R
Scarlet MX3R	Red MX8G	Red MX5B	Red MX8B	Magenta MXB
Rubine MX8A	Violet MX4RA	Violet MX2B	Blue MX3R	Blue MX2RA
Blue MX8A	Blue MXG	Blue MX4GD	Turquoise MXG	Blue MX5RA
Green MX3G	Green MXG	Green MX7B	Green MX8D	Olive MX6D
Navy MX4RD	Brown MX2GA	Brown MX2RA	Brown MX5BR	Grey MXB
Black MX2R	Black MXG	Yellow Ochre	Burnt Orange	Moroccan Red
Dusky Violet	Ultramarine	Lichen	Jade Green	Aubergine

If you intend to purchase all your dyes from the same supplier, you will soon get to recognize the various colour names which are associated with the various codes and will be able to order by name. If you buy from various suppliers, you may find that different suppliers call dyes of a particular code by a different colour name than your previous supplier. In this case, it is better to order those dyes you require by code rather than name to ensure you get the colour you are expecting.

Chemicals - Washing and Fixing

There are a wide range of chemicals on the market which can be used in dyeing. I only use two:

- **Synthrapol** - a strong detergent.
- **Soda Ash** - a dye fixative.

Many home dyers also use urea in their work. This is a wetting agent which can help your fabric absorb more dye and it can be useful in very dry climates. As I live in the UK, with its constantly changing climate and plentiful rainfall, I have never had any need of urea.

Synthrapol

Synthrapol is a strong, non-alkaline detergent which is readily available from dye suppliers. It is very useful for washing fabric that is not PFD (Prepared for Dyeing and Printing) as it will remove any sizing or other treatments that the fabric may have been subjected to. It is also incredibly useful for washing your fabric after dyeing and rinsing as it gets rid of any loose dye particles which have not bonded with the fibres. This will prevent bleeding in the future and boost colour-fastness.

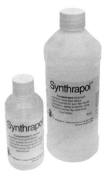

Soda Ash

Soda Ash is used as a dye fixative in that it helps the dye molecules permanently bond to the fibres during the curing (or batching) process. It is available from dye suppliers and I had been buying it for some years, at considerable expense, in 5kg tubs, until my kindly dye advisor told me that I could use washing soda instead. It is just as effective, available at my local supermarket, and considerably cheaper.

Equipment and Accessories

You will need very little specialist equipment to get started in your home-dyeing. Remember that once you have used them for dyeing, however, you will no longer be able to use them for food.

Keep it Simple

Dyeing is one of those gratifying hobbies in that it does not need specialist equipment to ensure success. In fact, it needs very little equipment at all, and that it does need is usually readily available at your local discount store or supermarket. You may find you have a lot of the list I am about to give you in your kitchen cupboards. This is fine. But remember that once you have used them for dyeing, you will no longer be able to use them for food preparation.

Rubber Gloves

Household gloves are available in a range of thicknesses, depending on how messy the job you want to use them for. But I use the standard dishwashing grade and find them adequate protection. I did buy a pack of disposable latex gloves, thinking I could just throw them away after each session. But as they only came up as far as my wrists and didn't have any cuffs, they were pretty useless.

Mask

This is the one item of equipment you should not skimp on. Dye particles are very fine and light and the softest breeze can cause them to become airborne. They MUST not be ingested or inhaled. I am not particularly prone to respiratory conditions but after just one ill-judged, mask-free dyeing session I was unwell for several weeks with a sore chest and cough.

Always use a mask that will protect you from fine particles. I like to use one with a central valve as this stops my glasses steaming up while I'm measuring out the dye powder. You only need to keep it on while working with dye in powder form, unless you are particularly susceptible to the mild fumes that mixed dyes give off.

Always ensure that you replace the lids on the containers of dye powder as soon as you have measured out the required amount.

Jugs

I like to mix my dyes in plastic jugs and keep them there until I have finished my dyeing session. Many people like to decant the mixed dye into old water or soft drink bottles and there is no doubt that this reduces the risk of spillage. But a plastic jug, with a good spout, is far easier to pour accurately from than a drinks bottle. If you have any left over after your session you can easily cover the top with food wrap and store it somewhere cool. Unless you have a dedicated fridge for dyeing supplies, and most of us don't, I wouldn't recommend storing it in your kitchen fridge.

I have three 1 litre (35 fl oz or 4 cups) jugs for mixing up the individual colours. You can see how the ones in the picture have become stained from so much use, but I always know which one to use for which colour now. I also have a larger 2 litre (70 fl oz or approx 8 cups) which is handy for measuring out the soaking water before I add the washing soda.

I use a small, clear plastic jug of 250ml (8 fl oz or approx 1 cup) for mixing the liquid dyes together before pouring into the plastic bags – but more about that later…

Plastic Drinking Cups

There is a wide range of cheap plastic drinking cups available and they normally come in packs of 50 or 100, or they do if you buy them online. I like to use those which are a popular size for beer and hold about 600ml (20 fl oz or 2 ½ cups). As they are not too narrow at the base they should remain quite stable when filled with wet fabric.

Plastic Spoons

These are invaluable for mixing dyes and they are so cheap and readily available that you don't mind throwing them away when they get a little the worse for wear.

Measuring Spoons, Wooden Spoons and Tongs

A standard set of cook's spoons, either in plastic or stainless steel, is all you need for measuring dye. In the UK these normally consist of a tablespoon (15ml), a dessertspoon (10ml), a teaspoon (5ml) and ½ teaspoon (2.5ml).

Wooden spoons are available in very basic shapes and as they are going to get stained, this is all you need. Make sure they are the long handled type. They are useful for stirring the washing soda into your bucket of warm water ready for fabric soaking.

I am mature enough to remember when washday meant battling with the ubiquitous twin-tub and took all day. My mother had several pairs of long, wooden tongs held together with a metal hinge, which she used for sloshing the boiling hot washing from the washing tank to the spin dryer. Some people still like to use them for retrieving pieces of fabric from the soaking liquid to transfer to the dye, but I prefer to use my rubber-gloved hands.

Plastic Bags

As I make craft kits for my website, I always have a stock of sturdy, resealable plastic bags. I thought it would make economic sense to use these for my dyeing and then rinse them out ready for the next session. Bad idea. I found that the bags leaked a little at the edges of the sealing strip, were almost impossible to open while wearing rubber gloves and deteriorated quite quickly after only one or two uses. So now I buy the bog-standard supermarket freezer bags on a roll, knot the top after adding my fabric and dye and just snip the knot off when I'm ready to rinse. Cheap and easy.

Bucket and Lid

A bucket with a close-fitting lid is ideal for soaking your fabrics in washing soda. When my daughter decided that terry towelling nappies were more trouble than they were worth, for my small grandson, she gave me the nappy bucket that was no longer needed. It is an ideal size and shape for my soaking operations, strong, stable-based and with a sturdy handle and lid. The lid prevents spillage and when you leave your fabrics to soak for a few days, it is a good idea to cover them up to contain the mild fumes from the washing soda and to stop any unwanted dust and debris falling in.

Plastic Trays

It is a good idea to buy a couple of large plastic trays with 2" edges all round. Large cat litter trays, if you can find them, are ideal. I use these to stack my bags of fabric in for curing or batching. I did used to put them in plastic buckets but worried about any leaks that might contaminate other bags of fabrics. Now I lay the filled bags out in one or two layers, in the trays, in batches of colour.

Part 2: The Dyeing Process

Get everything prepared for your first session.

 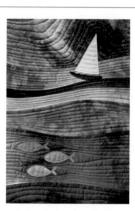  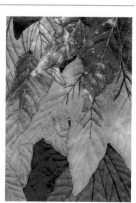

Keeping Records

If you want to be able to reproduce a range of repeatable colours, keeping accurate records is a must. Otherwise, you will soon get fed up with not being able to quite reproduce a particularly appealing colour, because you're relying on your memory.

Is Record-Keeping Really Necessary?

Maybe Not...

I am probably not the best person in the world to answer this question, but, as I am the author of this book, I will try.

As my long-suffering partner will testify, I am generally useless at record-keeping in all walks of life and generally leave such tasks until I can avoid them no longer.

I started dyeing as I was fascinated by the prospect of being able to make all sorts of unusual and unexpected colours. I do sell my fabrics to my sewing and website customers but always stipulate that each piece is a one-off and will never be repeated exactly – in either patterning or shade. This has never been a problem and customers are generally pleased to acquire something unique, even if it is just a piece of home-dyed fabric. So, apart from a few half-hearted attempts at keeping records of my dyed fabric collections, I have never recorded my recipes and methods. I firmly believe that that's what makes each dyeing session as exciting as the last.

But on the Other Hand...

However, if you want to turn your dyeing into a business supplying customers with repeatable colours, and this is probably necessary if you have photographs of the fabric on your website and don't want to be updating it every time you have a dyeing session, then you will probably need to keep records. They don't need to be complicated.

You could just draw a circle of diameter 7-8" and divide it into 12 equal segments. Photocopy a few onto printer card, punch some holes in them and store them in a loose-leaf folder. When you cut your fabrics for dyeing, make sure you cut them just a little larger to allow a large enough trimming to stick in each segment. Different dyeing operations may call for different recording methods. But whatever method you use, keep it simple, or you will soon get fed up with it.

Stage 1 – Preparing Your Fabric

How you cut your fabric depends on whether you want to a dye a little or a lot.

Cutting Your Fabric

When I have a dyeing session, I know it is going to take a while – at least a day. But if I extend the time I allow for dyeing to two days, I can potentially increase the number of pieces I can dye from 12 to 120. That's ten times the output for twice the time.

But you may not want 120 pieces of dyed fabric and, if this is your first attempt at the dyeing process, it is probably best to start with 12.

If you are fully confident that your efforts will result in the rainbow of fabulous shades that you have always dreamed of and want to take full advantage of that confidence, I will be giving some tips on cutting a large number of fat quarters quickly.

What Size Pieces?

I am not one for experimenting for the sake of it. If I am prepared to invest time, energy and funds into a particular project, I want something usable at the end of it, not just a collection of swatches that I can admire and post photos of on Facebook.

Many of the books I have read on home dyeing suggest starting with a fat eighth (20" x 10" or 8cm x 4cm) but what can you make with that? At least a fat quarter can be turned into a book cover, a laundry bag or a goodly number of patchwork squares.

There are numerous ideas for using fat quarters of dyed fabrics in the second book of my 'How to…' series – 'How to Sew With Confidence' and I will also be giving you a few ideas later on in this book.

So I would recommend that for your first attempt at a colour wheel, described in *Part 3*, you just stick to cutting out 12 fat quarters. You will actually need to cut them to 20" squares to allow:

- for shrinkage
- a little spare to paste into your record sheet.

> **Note**
> If you can find one, a 20½" quilter's square is very useful for this. See the Supplier's chapter for where to get one. If you can't find or don't want to purchase one, a quilter's 24" ruler will suffice, but is a little more difficult to hold steady!

Going for Bust

If like me, you are so confident that it is all going to turn out fine and you are going to dye more than 12 pieces, here's what to do.

> **Note**
> If you can see yourself dyeing a lot of fabric, it is much cheaper and more convenient to buy it on the roll.

I am assuming that you are cutting from a 60" (150cm) bolt of fabric. You will need either a 20½" quilters rule or a 6" x 24" quilters rule and a metre or yardstick (or a long piece of straight wooden batting. To cut from the roll:

1. Lay your fabric roll (so the fabric is unrolling from the bottom of the roll) at the back of a table long enough to accommodate its length and at least 30" wide. If you don't have such a table, use the floor.

2. Unroll at least 30" of the fabric.

3. If the cut edge of your fabric is not straight, line up your 20½" square against one of the finished edges of the fabric and the metre rule underneath resting on the lower edge of the square. If you are using a 6" x 24" ruler, line up one of the short edges with a finished edge.

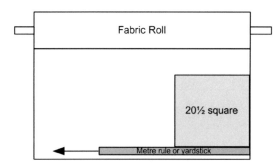

4 Using tailor's chalk, draw a line against the underside of the metre rule. Move the square to the opposite side of the fabric roll with the metre rule underneath, lined up with the line you drew, and continue the line all the way across the fabric.

5 Once you have straightened the cut edge, place your 20½" square in the centre of the unrolled fabric lining up one side with the cut edge. If you are using a 24" x 6" ruler, position it so roughly 21" is on the cloth and one short edge is resting against the wooden ruler.

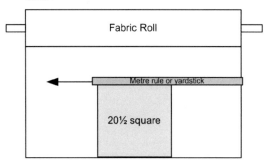

6 Place a metre rule or yardstick (or even a long piece of wooden battening) so it is resting on the top edge of the square or ruler.

7 Take a piece of coloured tailor's chalk and draw a line along the top of the wooden ruler, keeping the square or quilter's rule steady and sliding the wooden ruler across the top edge, until your line reaches the full width of the fabric.

8 Cut along the line.

Note

When cutting, you can use scissors, which, if they are large and sharp enough should just glide through the fabric. You can also nick the edge of the fabric at the line and rip it, but this does produce a lot of loose threads and, if the fabric grain is slightly skewed (as it sometimes is) you will find yourself wasting fabric. You can use a rotary cutter, if you don't mind moving your cutting mat around to save damaging the table and blade!

9 Remove the quilter's rule and wooden ruler or batten and the cut piece of fabric.

10 Unroll another 30" of fabric and place the piece you have just cut on top, lining up the raw edges.

11 Cut another piece the same as the first.

12 Continue cutting strips of fabric until you have enough for the number of fat quarters you want. Remember that if your fabric is 60" wide you will get 3 fat quarters (or 20" squares) out of each strip.

13 When you have sufficient strips of fabric, remove the fabric roll from the table.

14 Stack three strips on the table, measure it into three 20" sections and cut.

15 Continue until you have the required number of fat quarters.

Pre-Soaking Your Fabric

Your fabric must be pre-soaked in a solution containing a fixative before dyeing. If you miss out this step, your fabric, once immersed, in the dye, and cured for the recommended time, will appear to have absorbed the dye. But when rinsed and scoured in the washing machine, most of the dye will wash out.

The Fixative

For pre-soaking fabric, I use common, household washing soda. This is readily available in most large supermarkets and hardware shops. If you can't find it, you can buy soda ash from dye suppliers.

Now if you have decided to dye more than 12 pieces for your first session, it is unlikely they will all fit in your average-sized bucket, so you will need to do your soaking, and consequently your dyeing, in stages.

When I have my 120-piece dyeing sessions I divide the 120 pieces by 12 (12 colour steps) and get 10. So I will have 12 loads of 10 pieces to soak. This has the advantage that I will only be dealing with one step of the colour wheel at a time so there will be less chance for confusion.

You can use the same soaking liquid time and time again but it is inevitable that some will be lost when removing fabric pieces. This is easily remedied by occasionally adding a little more washing soda and hot water to top up your solution.

Mixing the Fixative Solution

To mix your pre-soaking fixative solution:

1   Put on your rubber gloves and an apron.

2   Into a standard-sized bucket, with or without a lid, put 3 litres (5 pints) of hot water and 2 litres (3½ pints) of cold water.

3   Measure out 8 oz of washing soda (or soda ash) into a plastic cup.

> **Note**
> It is a good idea to use a set of cheap digital scales for measuring your dyeing ingredients. Just put a plastic cup on the scales, switch on and fill the cup to the required measurement.

4   Using an old wooden spoon to stir, pour the washing soda into the water in a steady stream and mix until dissolved.

Adding Your Fabric

To ensure that each piece of fabric absorbs enough fixative:

1   Peel one fat quarter off your stack of fabric and using the wooden spoon or a gloved hand, push it down into the solution.

2   Repeat with the remaining fabric, ensuring each piece is completely immersed and swished around in the solution. This gets

more difficult the more pieces you add, but just keep turning the fabric around in the bucket until it is completely soaked.

3   Leave to soak for at least half an hour.

> **Note**
> If your dyeing session is interrupted at this stage, as often happens, don't worry. The fabric will be fine in the solution for up to a week. If you do need to leave it for more than a few hours, cover with a lid or old tea towel.

Stage 2 - Mixing Your Dyes

Observe a few safety precautions and a bit of good housekeeping and your dye mixing will be simple.

Safety Reminders

You are probably tired of reading about safety by now, but I cannot stress strongly enough how important it is to wear a mask, suitable for protection against fine dust particles, when measuring out dye in powder form.

- **While Procion dyes are not normally considered hazardous on the skin, people with sensitive skin or any pre-existing skin conditions, should always wear rubber gloves when handling dyes in powder or liquid form.**

- **Ensure that all the containers and utensils that you use for dyeing are kept for that purpose only and are never used for food preparation or serving.**

- **Do not prepare foods on the same surface you have prepared dyes on. If you have no alternative to using your kitchen worktop, cover it with a large plastic sheet before each dyeing session.**

All the recipes and projects in this book are made using only red, blue, yellow and, occasionally, black. Each primary colour requires a different quantity of dye powder to water and these are detailed in the chapters detailing the various dyeing sessions.

Mixing the Dye Powder into a Solution

To ensure your dyes are thoroughly mixed:

1 Put on your mask, gloves and apron.

2 Using a dry teaspoon measure from a cooks set, scoop out a teaspoon of dye powder. Holding the teaspoon over the dye powder container, use the handle of a plastic spoon to level off the powder.

3 Place the powder into the bottom of a 1litre (2 pint) plastic jug.

> **Note:**
> Don't tip the powder in from the top as this will cause some particles to become airborne.

4 Add further dye powder until you have the correct amount for the colour you are mixing.

5 Firmly replace the lid on the dye powder container and return it to your storage area.

6 Add a little warm water to the dye powder and stir, with a plastic spoon, until you have a smooth paste.

7 Set your hot tap to run at a slow steady stream and keep stirring until the water reaches the correct level.

8 Give a final stir and set aside.

If you get interrupted at this stage, the dyes can be covered with cling film and stored in a cool place for several weeks. I don't recommend storing them in the fridge unless you have a separate fridge for the purpose, but a cool, frost free place will be fine. If you are worried about spillage – and you should be – you can either stand the jugs in a plastic box, high-sided enough to contain any accidents or decant each colour into a plastic bottle with a screw-on lid.

Stage 3 – Setting Up Your Equipment

Getting everything ready before you start will prevent panic and unnecessary mistakes.

Where to Dye

When you have a dyeing session, the one thing you will need most of, is water. Lots of it. You need it for mixing, constant gloved-hand washing (between stuffing your pieces of fabric into dye-filled bags and getting the next piece out of the pre-soaking liquid) and rinsing out your mopping-up cloth.

If you possibly can, set up your dye station next to a sink with a source of running water. It will make your life a whole lot easier.

Setting Out your Containers

However many pieces of fabric you have decided to dye in the first session; you will never need more than 12 plastic cups at one time. See the Equipment section for details of the best cups to use.

I am constantly aware of the risk of dye spillage. It is not dangerous, generally, but it is incredibly messy. It will be absorbed anything it touches and, on most things, will never fully wash out. Wear the oldest clothes you have and a long, plastic apron.

I like to set out my plastic cups in a plastic tray. This stops the inevitable small spillages travelling far and making contact with anything absorbent.

Try to make sure that the plastic cups you choose are reasonably stable as it is a real nuisance if they are constantly tipping over.

Plastic Bags

As I said in the Equipment section, you can either use re-sealable bags and wash them out after use, or you can go for the cheap supermarket, on-a-roll, type and throw them away after each use. Whatever you decide to use, you will need to line each cup with a bag, pushing it well down into the base and turning the edges over the rim.

Before you start, have ready your small plastic 250ml (1 cup) jug and a container of plastic spoons.

Cleaning up

It is a good idea to have a pack of disposable cloths and several rolls of kitchen paper. I get through at least one roll of kitchen paper for each session and have now started buying the 'Big' extra-absorbent brand so I only need one sheet per spillage instead of ripping off two or three.

If you are doing your dyeing in a carpeted area, it is a good idea to cover the area where you will be working with a non-slip plastic sheet. I have carpet tiles in my studio kitchen and, over the years, the corrosive action of the washing soda that I have been sloshing around, has made them quite threadbare.

Stage 4 - Immersing Your Fabric in the Dye

The patterning of your finished fabric will depend on how you immerse it into the dye solution.

The Best Way?

When I first started out in dyeing, I read as many books on the subject as I could get my hands on. In this subject, as in most other subjects, there are many schools of thought on how you should do things. In this book, I am sharing with you the methods that I have found to work for me. You may try these out and decide that there is a better way. That is progress and I encourage you to go ahead, discover your own methods and share them with those who want to learn. I would also be delighted if you would share them with me.

The Dye Bath

Dye bath is the term that is used for the dye solution that you have prepared in readiness for your dyeing session. The term 'bath' infers a large amount of solution such as is used in an industrial dyeing operation but, in reality, can mean any quantity. The quantities, for the dyeing sessions detailed in the following section, vary depending on the method and effects we are trying to achieve. This section merely details the method of immersing your fabric in the dye bath for maximum effect.

To Wring or Not to Wring?

Many of the dyeing books, and blogs, that I have read, tell me that I should transfer the pre-soaked fabric from the fixative solution to the dye bath while it is dripping – no wringing allowed. I can appreciate the theory behind this method. If the fabric is not wrung out it will retain more of the fixative and perhaps absorb more dye.

I, however, have found this not only incredibly wasteful – by the time you have transferred all of your 12 pieces from fixative to dye bath, most of

your solution will have disappeared – but also that the extra water dilutes the dye bath even further than intended.

So I wring out, quite firmly, saving my solution for the next batch of fabrics.

Dunking and Dyeing

Like many of the other operations in this book, there is no hard and fast way of inserting your fabric into the dye solution. This is my method and this will give a pleasing pattern resembling – I think – dappled light filtering through a forest of trees.

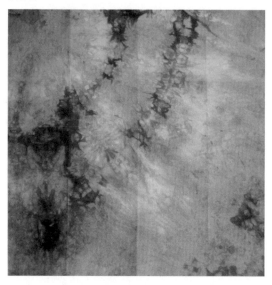

1   Wearing your rubber gloves, take one piece of pre-soaked fabric from your bucket of fixative solution and wring out firmly, into the bucket.

2   Stretch the fabric out, corner to corner, like a small spear and insert it into the dye point first. Of course the point will start to collapse as soon as it touches the base of the plastic bag. But keep pushing it in until the whole piece is pressed into the base of the cup.

3   Holding the top of the bag, lift it out of the cup and shake lightly so the fabric 'sausage' is lying along the bottom seam of the bag.

4   Grasp the fabric through the bag and massage firmly, pushing the dye solution up and through the fabric several times. Take care that you don't push the solution over the top of the bag.

5   If you are putting two pieces of fabric into each bag – see *Getting More From Each Dye Session* - now is the time to add the second piece.

> **Note**
> The first piece of fabric into the dye will absorb the majority of the dye particles and will always be the most deeply coloured. But there are usually many more particles than can be absorbed by one piece, so I always pop a second one into the bag. Bear in mind that, although the second piece will be the same hue or colour, it will be several shades lighter.

6   Massage the fabrics as before, carefully turning them around in the dye until all parts have been immersed.

7   Seal the bag firmly, either by pressing together the resealable strips or, if you have gone the cheap and cheerful route, knotting the top.

8   Lay the bags of fabric and dye, in one layer, in a large plastic tray.

> **Note:**
> I like to keep bags of similar colours together in the tray so, if there is any leakage between bags, it is unlikely to cause too much damage.

Curing or Batching

Most Procion dyes will be cured and ready to rinse within three hours, but some, especially turquoise (Cerulean Blue) and those containing turquoise – type dyes, will need 24 hours curing time. The fabric needs to be kept warm while curing. If you have an airing cupboard with shelving, this is an ideal place.

In the summer, I cover my trays of fabric with black bin bags and put them in the greenhouse for the recommended curing time.

Stage 5 – Finishing Off

Rinsing and scouring your fabric thoroughly will prevent colour runs in the future. Once done you will then need to trim and iron your fabric to prepare it for use.

Rinsing

The Importance of Pre-Rinsing

When I first started dyeing, and subsequently rinsing, I thought it would be a simple matter of emptying the bags of cured fabric into my automatic washing machine, setting it to 'Rinse and Spin' and, in 15 minutes it would all be ready for scouring. Not so...

Even if, like me, you put two pieces of fabric in each dye bag, there will still be loose, unused dye molecules floating around at the end of the curing time. And if like me, you gaily empty these bags into the washing machine, that unused dye is going to leach into all the other pieces of fabric that are already in there. Result – technicolour disaster!

Pre-Rinse Method

The most efficient, and least messy, way of pre-rinsing, is as follows:

1   Don a full-length plastic apron and your rubber gloves.

2   At the sink, lay a large, plastic dish drainer on the draining board and the tray of fabrics on the opposite side of the sink. Remove the washing up bowl from the sink.

3   From the tray, choose 3-4 bags of fabric of the same colour range. Open each one in turn and pour carefully into the sink.

4   Set the cold tap running in a slow, steady stream.

5   The fabrics will be compacted into balls so pull each piece apart so it is fully open.

6   Swish the fabrics around in the water until most of the residual dye has washed away.

7   Put the plug into the sink outlet and allow the sink to half-fill. Swish and squeeze the fabrics to get out as much dye as possible.

8   Drain the water away and repeat the previous steps until the water is looking quite clear.

9   Wring each piece of fabric out and place on the dish drainer.

10 When you have rinsed all the fabrics from one colour range, put them in the washing machine and set it to 'Rinse and Spin'.

11 When the programme is finished, take the fabrics out, untangle them and trim off any loose threads.

Note:
If you don't have a '**Rinse and Spin**' setting on your washing machine, you will need to do a few more rinsing sessions at the sink, until the water is perfectly clear, before the fabric is ready for scouring. Some machines, like the one shown below have separate '**Rinse**' and '**Spin**' settings and you will need to run the '**Rinse**' followed by the '**Spin**' programme.

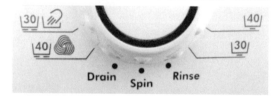

Scouring

Scouring, a term which sounds like it should involve a lot of elbow grease, is the washing of the fabric in a strong detergent. This ensures that any loose dye molecules, which are clinging to the fabric but have not bonded to the fibres, are washed away. This is a very important step as, if these molecules are allowed to remain they may cause colour runs in future washes. This could be very upsetting if you have spent ages, incorporating the fabric into a project.

Once you have thoroughly rinsed and spun your fabrics in colour-range batches, you can put them all into the machine for scouring.

To scour your fabrics:

1 Place your rinsed and spun fabrics back into the machine and add 1 teaspoon of Synthrapol for every 12 fat quarters (or 2 metres) of fabric.

2 Set the machine to a 40°C programme.

Drying Your Fabric

If you are impatient to use your new dyed fabric, you can tumble-dry it. But I find that machine-drying makes the fabric very creased and harder to iron – especially if you forget to take it out before it is bone dry! I prefer to give each piece a good shake when it comes out of the washing machine and then hang it on a clothes airer to dry naturally.

Trimming and Ironing

If you are dyeing your fabrics to sell, either to your sewing class customers, in your shop, or online, it is a good idea to present them at their best by trimming, ironing and folding them into neat regular packages. If they are for your own use, it is still nicer, and more inspirational to see them lined up on a shelf, or in baskets, rather than just heaped in an unruly pile.

Now this is where it is very useful to have dried your fabrics naturally, rather than tumble drying them. If they are very creased, you will need to iron them, with a hot steam iron, before you can trim them. But, if they have been air dried, they will be quite flat already, so you can trim them and then iron and fold all in one operation.

Trimming

If you are selling your fabrics as fat quarters, you will need to ensure that they are at least 20" x 18" in size. I always try and cut mine as close to 20" square as possible. You can use the trimmings to paste into your records sheet.

Ironing and Folding

A good steam iron is a boon when preparing dyed cotton fabrics. If you have a steam generator iron with a separate water tank, so much the better. Whichever you have:

1 Set your iron to the highest temperature and switch it to steam.

2 Iron each piece thoroughly.

3 While it is still on the ironing board, fold two opposite sides of the fabric square into the centre, then fold in half, so the folded edges meet.

4 Fold each of the raw edges into the middle to form a neat square.

Part 3: Dyeing a 12-Step Colour Wheel

Now we get to the practical bit and dye our first basic colour wheel.

 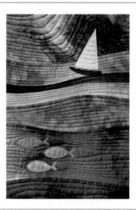  

A Bit About Colour Theory

Don't be afraid of colour – it can change your life. You will need to understand a few basics about colours and how they are related before you begin dyeing fabric. Once you understand the basics, you will then be able to extend and customise your own dyeing projects.

Embrace Colour

Colour is one of those things that many of us a terrified of. We claim we have no sense of colour, that we don't know which colours go together and we don't know which colours suit us. But, regardless of all these claims, most of us do know what we like, in terms of colour and collections of colour.

The Colour Wheel

The colour wheel is a very useful tool for organizing the colours of the spectrum:

- Red
- Orange
- Yellow
- Green
- Blue
- Violet

The wheel is usually presented in a circular format which makes it easier to see the relationships between the colours.

Colour wheels are available in various levels of complexity. Some showing just the main colours of the spectrum and some showing the secondary and tertiary colours too.

The one I have has a rotating central wheel with a window with an arrow above it. When the arrow is pointed to the area between two colours, the result of mixing these colours is shown in the window.

Primary Colours

The primary colours are those that are used as the base of all other colours and cannot be mixed. They are Red, Blue and Yellow.

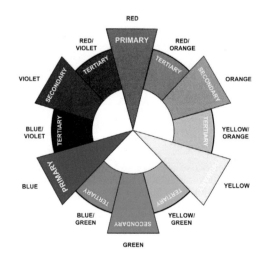

Secondary Colours

Secondary colours are produced when two primary colours are mixed together. Green, Orange and Violet are secondary colours.

Tertiary Colours

These are the colours produced when you mix two secondary colours or one primary and one secondary together:

- Red/Orange
- Red/Violet
- Blue/Violet
- Blue/Green
- Yellow/Green
- Yellow/Orange

Complementary Colours

Complementary colours are those which are *opposite* each other on the colour wheel. Examples of these are:

- Yellow and Violet

- Green and Red

- Orange and Blue

Sometimes these colours can look good together but often they are too strong to sit comfortably side by side.

Harmonious Colours

Harmonious colours are those that sit *next to* each other on the colour wheel, such as Violet, Red and Orange.

Be Brave...

Don't be afraid of colour. Learn the basic terms and theory and refer to your colour wheel often. You will very soon get to know what works and what doesn't but most important of all, have fun experimenting.

33

The 12-Step "Pure" Colour Wheel Recipe

Having read the previous sections on preparing your fabrics, dyes and equipment, you will now be itching to try your hand at dyeing for real. This section provides instructions on exactly how to create your first hand-dyed colour wheel.

What You Will Need

For this colour wheel I have used the most basic primary colours which will give the most intense (or purest) results:

- Red MX-8B
- Blue MX-R
- Yellow MX-8G

Pure Colour Wheel

For this particular colour wheel you will need the following quantities of dye powder to water:

Red Dyes

For red dye, you will need two level teaspoons of dye powder to 500ml (2 cups or 16 fl.oz) of water.

Blue Dye

For blue dye, you will need four level teaspoons of dye powder to 500ml (2 cups or 16 fl.oz) of water.

Yellow Dye

For yellow dye, you will need six level teaspoons of dye powder to 500ml (2 cups or 16 fl.oz) of water.

Dyeing Your Colour Wheel

To dye your first colour wheel:

1   Referring to *Stage 1 - Preparing Your Fabric*, cut 12 pieces 20" x 20" and soak your fabric pieces for at least 30 minutes.

2   Referring to *Stage 2 - Mixing Your Dyes* for specific mixing instructions of dye powder into water, and the specific quantities required for this wheel, mix 500ml of red, blue and yellow dyes in separate plastic jugs. Set aside.

3   Referring to *Stage 3 - Setting Up Your Equipment*, set out 12 large plastic cups in a plastic tray and line each cup with a plastic bag.

4   Referring to *Stage 4 - Immersing Your Fabric in the Dye*, measure the dyes into each of the 12 cups. Wring out and immerse one piece of fabric in each cup. Then stack and cure the bags of dyed fabric for at least 3 hours.

> **Note:**
> If you have used turquoise or cerulean blue in your colour wheel or if any of your dyes contain these colours, set them aside to cure for 24 hours.

5   Referring to *Stage 5 - Finishing Off*, rinse and scour your fabric. Then trim and iron to prepare your fabric for use.

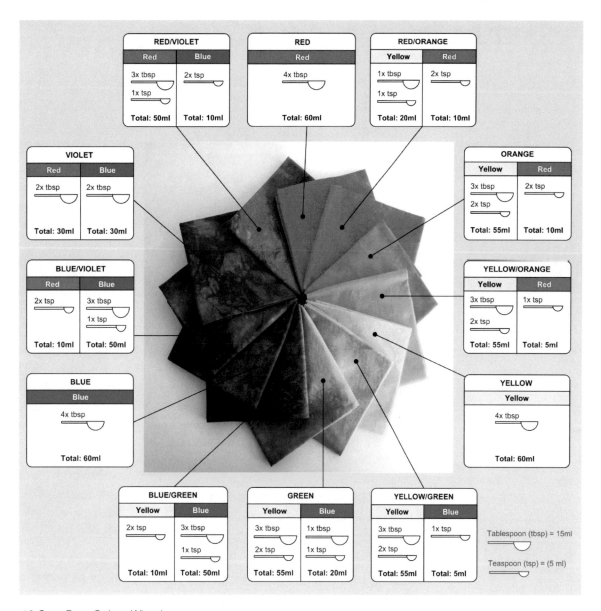

RED/VIOLET

Red	Blue
3x tbsp	2x tsp
1x tsp	
Total: 50ml	**Total: 10ml**

RED

Red
4x tbsp
Total: 60ml

RED/ORANGE

Yellow	Red
1x tbsp	2x tsp
1x tsp	
Total: 20ml	**Total: 10ml**

VIOLET

Red	Blue
2x tbsp	2x tbsp
Total: 30ml	**Total: 30ml**

ORANGE

Yellow	Red
3x tbsp	2x tsp
2x tsp	
Total: 55ml	**Total: 10ml**

BLUE/VIOLET

Red	Blue
2x tsp	3x tbsp
	1x tsp
Total: 10ml	**Total: 50ml**

YELLOW/ORANGE

Yellow	Red
3x tbsp	1x tsp
2x tsp	
Total: 55ml	**Total: 5ml**

BLUE

Blue
4x tbsp
Total: 60ml

YELLOW

Yellow
4x tbsp
Total: 60ml

BLUE/GREEN

Yellow	Blue
2x tsp	3x tbsp
	1x tsp
Total: 10ml	**Total: 50ml**

GREEN

Yellow	Blue
3x tbsp	1x tbsp
2x tsp	1x tsp
Total: 55ml	**Total: 20ml**

YELLOW/GREEN

Yellow	Blue
3x tbsp	1x tsp
2x tsp	
Total: 55ml	**Total: 5ml**

Tablespoon (tbsp) = 15ml

Teaspoon (tsp) = (5 ml)

12-Step Pure Colour Wheel

Alternative Colour Wheel Recipes

By using different primary colours you will dramatically change the look of your colour wheel. We've only just begun...

Using Different Primaries

In the first 12-step colour wheel, I used the most basic primaries that would produce the most intense colours. I did this deliberately, as I found the resulting colours are so exciting that I couldn't wait to try out more combinations of dyes to see the results.

These were the colours I used:

- Red MX-8B
- Blue MX-R
- Yellow MX-8G

The reason for the intensity and clarity of the resulting colours is that the primaries I used were as pure as possible. The Red MX-8B is reddish-blue and the Blue MX-R is bluish red. As there is no other colour involved they will produce a set of lively purples and violets. The Yellow MX-8G is also pure yellow, so, when mixed with the red will produce vibrant oranges and when mixed with the blue will produce verdant greens.

Of course the most obvious way of obtaining different results is to change the primary colours that are mixed to produce the colour wheels. But you don't have to go as far as changing all three primaries. By just substituting one of them for another, you will dramatically change the look of your colour wheel.

Singing the Blues...

By substituting the Blue MX-R for Turquoise MX-G, we will be changing the bluish-red to bluish-yellow, but we are still not introducing any other colours into the mix. In fact, by increasing the yellow content, we are brightening the colours even further. You will discover that the section of your colour wheel in which blue is added to the mix will be changed to a bright zingy set of lime greens, turquoise blues and luscious violets. The section in which reds and yellows are used will remain the same, until you place them next to the remainder of the wheel. The new brighter section will appear to brighten the whole wheel. This is useful if you plan to use the whole wheel together in one project.

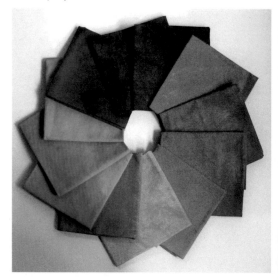

Brights Colour Wheel using Turquoise MX-G in Place of Blue MX-G

All Change

Now changing all of the primaries will have a huge effect on your colour wheel. You could try a red which is less blue or one which is greener. You could try a blue which is more yellow than red, and you could try a yellow whose acidity is softened by a hint of redness.

The reds which I always have on my shelf are:

- Red MX-8B (the purest)
- Cerise Red MX 5B
- Intense Red MX-GN
- Scarlet Red MX-3G

The blues I always have on my shelf are:

36

- Royal Blue MX-R (the purest)
- Indigo Navy-MX 2G
- Turquoise MX-G

And the yellows which I like to keep to hand:

- Acid Lemon MX-8G (the purest)
- Golden Yellow MX-3R

Not Bright...But Beautiful

Bear in mind that when you change your primaries to those which have other colour influences, you are introducing another colour into what was initially a pure mix. This will have the effect of dulling your colours.

Remember what happened in primary school when you mixed all the paint colours together hoping for a new and wonderful shade – and all you got was mud? This is an extreme example but illustrates that throwing more colours into the mix will take away the brightness of the basic colour wheel. If you are a lover of landscapes and country colours, this is a change you will welcome as you reveal a world of earthy, natural hues.

In the following pages are a few of my favourite recipes for alternative colour wheels and ones which I use most often.

"Back to Nature" Colour Wheel Recipe

This recipe will give you slightly duller reds, oranges and yellows but will also provide the colours of leaves and trees, the blues of deepest oceans and the ripe shades of sun-kissed plums, cherries and aubergines.

What You Will Need

For this 12-step colour wheel you will need:

- Intense Red MX-GN
- Indigo Navy MX-2G
- Golden Yellow MX-3R

Back To Nature Colour Wheel

For this colour wheel you will need the same quantities of dye powder to water, as we used for the pure colour wheel:

Red Dyes

For red dye, you will need two level teaspoons of dye powder to 500ml (2 cups or 16 fl.oz) of water.

Blue Dye

For blue dye, you will need four level teaspoons of dye powder to 500ml (2 cups or 16 fl.oz) of water.

Yellow Dye

For yellow dye, you will need six level teaspoons of dye powder to 500ml (2 cups or 16 fl.oz) of water.

Dyeing Your Colour Wheel

To dye your colour wheel, we will proceed in the same way as for the pure colour wheel:

1   Referring to *Stage 1 - Preparing Your Fabric,* cut 12 pieces 20" x 20". and soak your fabric pieces for at least 30 minutes.

2   Referring to *Stage 2 - Mixing Your Dyes* for specific mixing instructions of dye powder into water, and the specific dye recipes on this page, mix 500ml of red, blue and yellow dyes in separate plastic jugs. Set aside.

3   Referring to *Stage 3 - Setting Up Your Equipment,* set out 12 large plastic cups in a plastic tray and line each cup with a plastic bag.

4   Referring to *Stage 4 - Immersing Your Fabric in the Dye,* measure the dyes into each of the 12 cups. Wring out and immerse one piece of fabric in each cup. Then stack and cure the bags of dyed fabric for at least 3 hours.

5   Referring to *Stage 5 - Finishing Off,* rinse and scour your fabric. Then trim and iron to prepare your fabric for use.

How to Dye Your Own Fabric   Part 3: Dyeing a 12-Step Colour Wheel

"Under the Sun" Colour Wheel Recipe

While I've never visited the Australian outback or the scorched deserts of Namibia, I think the colours of this next wheel are those you would find in some of the hottest places on earth. The yellows are those of shifting sand dunes and dusty roads, the greens those of struggling vegetation and wandering tumbleweeds and the blues and violets – once bright – have been bleached and aged by the relentless heat.

What You Will Need

These are the primary dyes you will need.

- Wine Red
- Indigo Navy MX-2G
- Golden Yellow MX-3R

Under the Sun Colour Wheel

You will notice that there is only one change from the previous wheel and that is the red, which is a Wine colour. This dye has no code as it is no longer available commercially – at least from my supplier. I have been told that it was originally manufactured using Copper Sulphate but as that is no longer allowed in dye preparations, so we have to mix it ourselves.

Before mixing the Wine colour you will need to prepare the red, blue and yellow dye mixes.

For this colour wheel you will need the same quantities of dye powder to water, as we used for the pure colour wheel:

Red Dyes

For red dye, you will need two level teaspoons of dye powder to 500ml (2 cups or 16 fl.oz) of water.

Blue Dye

For blue dye, you will need four level teaspoons of dye powder to 500ml (2 cups or 16 fl.oz) of water.

Yellow Dye

For yellow dye, you will need six level teaspoons of dye powder to 500ml (2 cups or 16 fl.oz) of water.

Mixing the Wine Colour

Mixing the Wine colour is a simple process and to make it you will need the following proportions of mixed dye solutions:

- 85% Intense Red MX-GN
- 5% Indigo Navy MX-2G
- 10% Golden Yellow MX-3R

So if you wanted to mix 500ml of Wine red you would need:

- 425ml of Intense Red MX-GN
- 25ml of Indigo Navy MX-2G
- 50ml of Golden Yellow MX-3R

A small change, you might think. But try it, You will be awed by the results.

Dyeing Your Colour Wheel

To dye your colour wheel, we will proceed in the same way as for the pure colour wheel:

39

1 Referring to *Stage 1 - Preparing Your Fabric,* cut 12 pieces 20" x 20". and soak your fabric pieces for at least 30 minutes.

2 Referring to *Stage 2 - Mixing Your Dyes* for specific mixing instructions of dye powder into water and the specific dye recipes in this section, mix 500ml of red, blue and yellow dyes in separate plastic jugs. Set aside.

3 Referring to *Stage 3 - Setting Up Your Equipment,* set out 12 large plastic cups in a plastic tray and line each cup with a plastic bag.

4 Referring to *Stage 4 - Immersing Your Fabric in the Dye,* measure the dyes into each of the 12 cups. Wring out and immerse one piece of fabric in each cup. Then stack and cure the bags of dyed fabric for at least 3 hours.

5 Referring to *Stage 5 - Finishing Off,* rinse and scour your fabric. Then trim and iron to prepare your fabric for use.

"Neutral" Shades Recipe

It's quite difficult to define what a neutral colour really is. It doesn't have a single hue, but many neutrals have shades of other colours in them. Just visit your nearest DIY store and you will see whole displays of neutral paints with evocative names such as apple white, dusted damson and cocoa powder.

Neutral but Not?

In fabric dyeing, we can create some very evocative neutrals that can provide the perfect background for the most vibrant of quilts.

They can also be used on their own to make a piece that reminds you of the natural world. The wonderful browns, golds and rusty reds, the evening-sky shades of mauve and dusky blue and the gentle greens of last year's vegetation.

A Range of 12 Neutral Shades

When I dyed neutral fabrics for sale in my workshops, they were always the first to go. There is something comforting and homely about them, something everyone is drawn to.

Getting Neutral Shades

Buying from Dye Suppliers

Dye suppliers stock a wide range of neutral shades such black, chestnut, charcoal and various degrees of brown.

Neutralizing by Adding Black

Obviously, adding black to any colour is going to make it darker. Even just a little can have a considerable dulling effect on the intensity of the colour. This is a technique that it used by many artists who call it neutralizing.

Making Your Own Neutrals

I think it is much more fun to make your own neutrals and, with just a small stock of primary colours, you can make a whole range of warm, mellow neutral shades. In the next section, I will show you how to make a small selection of neutral shades using basic, or pure, primary colours.

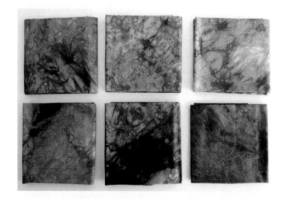

A Collection of Rich Woodland Shades Using Pure Primaries

Collection of Neutrals Using Mixed Primaries

Choosing Your Primaries

When you dye a standard 12-step colour wheel using three primaries, you can be fairly certain of the range of colours you are going to achieve. They may be a little brighter or duller, depending on the dyes you have chosen, but using the standard 12-step recipe, you know you are going to get the standard 12 hues.

Things, however, are a little different in neutral land. The dye recipes are different from the standard recipe, and the fact that we add all three primary colours at once can cause some quite startling results.

For this Woodland Collection, I have used the following primaries:

- Intense Red MX-GN
- Royal Blue MX-R
- Acid Lemon MX-8G

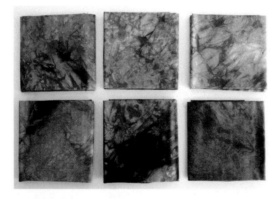

What You Will Need

For this selection of neutrals, you will need 6 fat quarters of pre-soaked fabric and 6 plastic bag lined cups.

For this particular colour exercise, you will need the following quantities of dye powder to water:

Red Dyes

For red dye, you will need 1½ level teaspoons of dye powder to 250ml (1 cups or 8 fl.oz) of water.

Blue Dye

For blue dye, you will need 1 level teaspoon of dye powder to 250ml (1 cups or 8 fl.oz) of water.

Yellow Dye

For yellow dye, you will need 1 level teaspoon of dye powder to 250ml (1 cups or 8 fl.oz) of water.

Dyeing Your Colour Wheel

To dye your colour wheel, we will proceed in the same way as for the pure colour wheel:

1 Referring to *Stage 1 - Preparing Your Fabric,* cut 12 pieces 20" x 20". and soak your fabric pieces for at least 30 minutes.

2 Referring to *Stage 2 - Mixing Your Dyes* for specific mixing instructions of dye powder into water, and referring to the specific dye ratio to water detailed above.

3 Referring to *Stage 3 - Setting Up Your Equipment,* set out 6 large plastic cups in a plastic tray and line each cup with a plastic bag.

4 Referring to *Stage 4 - Immersing Your Fabric in the Dye,* measure the dyes into each of the 6 cups. Wring out and immerse one piece of fabric in each cup. Then stack and cure the bags of dyed fabric for at least 3 hours.

5 Referring to *Stage 5 - Finishing Off,* rinse and scour your fabric. Then trim and iron to prepare your fabric for use

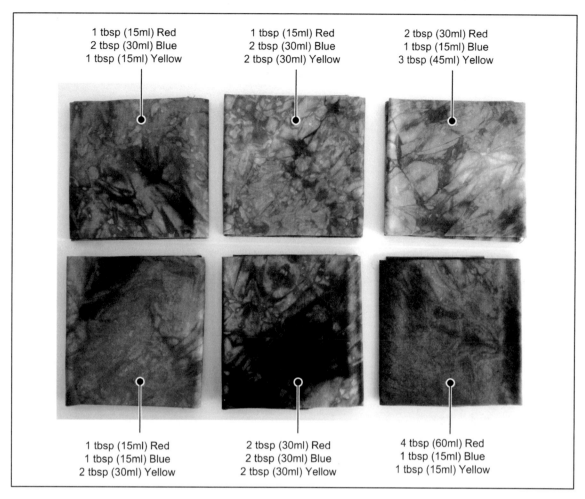

1 tbsp (15ml) Red
2 tbsp (30ml) Blue
1 tbsp (15ml) Yellow

1 tbsp (15ml) Red
2 tbsp (30ml) Blue
2 tbsp (30ml) Yellow

2 tbsp (30ml) Red
1 tbsp (15ml) Blue
3 tbsp (45ml) Yellow

1 tbsp (15ml) Red
1 tbsp (15ml) Blue
2 tbsp (30ml) Yellow

2 tbsp (30ml) Red
2 tbsp (30ml) Blue
2 tbsp (30ml) Yellow

4 tbsp (60ml) Red
1 tbsp (15ml) Blue
1 tbsp (15ml) Yellow

Neutral "Woodland Colours" Shades

Part 4: Getting More From Your Colour Wheels

How to get more colours, and more dyed fabric, from each dyeing process.

 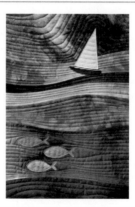  

Exploring Between the Steps of the Colour Wheel

Your colour wheel is bright and beautiful but may need a few gentle colours to tone it down. Let's look at what's hiding between those 12 steps.

Using the Fabrics in Your Colour Wheel

So you've dyed your 12-step colour wheel. You may have even tried all four different primary mixes. But what are you going to do with them?

If you're a patchworker or quilter, you may like to make a quilt. But using just the colours in the wheel might be a bit garish. After all, they're dramatically different from each other and may fight for attention in your project.

What you need is some other colours, something that will match those you've created but are not quite so dramatic. Those colours are there, just waiting to be discovered, in between the steps of your colour wheel.

The Missing Colours

My partner is an erstwhile water colour artist and tells me that the same problem, of too many bright colours, also occurs in painting. The method of mixing existing colours to produce those that are not too 'in your face' is called 'knocking-back'.

We are going to do a similar thing in dyeing – well the outcome is similar – but the process requires rather more mixing, measuring, curing and rinsing.

From Primary to Primary

The elusive colours are lurking in between the three primaries we used to create the original wheel. The original wheel currently has three steps between each primary colour:

- Blue to Red
- Red to Yellow
- Yellow to Blue

By gradually mixing each of these two primaries together we can achieve 7 steps. This will give you 24 colours in your wheel. This process is called a *two-colour dye run*.

Dyeing a Two-Colour Dye Run

To create a more gradual shift in colour from one primary to another, we will use the two-colour dye run to create 7 intermediate colour steps.

What You Will Need

For this two-colour dye run you will need 9 fat quarters of pre-soaked fabric and 9 plastic bag lined cups.

From Blue to Red

These are the dyes I used for the example shown below:

- Red MX-8B
- Blue MX-R

Blue to red two-colour dye run

The ratio of dye powder to water is the same as that given in the instructions for the 12-step colour wheel but for this exercise you will only need the red and blue dyes.

Red Dyes

For red dye, you will need two level teaspoons of dye powder to 500ml (2 cups or 16 fl.oz) of water.

Blue Dye

For blue dye, you will need four level teaspoons of dye powder to 500ml (2 cups or 16 fl.oz) of water.

Dyeing Your Two-Colour Dye Run

To dye your first two-colour dye run, proceed as follows:

1   Referring to *Stage 1 - Preparing Your Fabric,* cut 9 pieces 20" x 20". and soak your fabric pieces for at least 30 minutes.

2   Referring to *Stage 2 - Mixing Your Dyes* for specific mixing instructions of dye powder into water and the specific dye recipe in this section, mix 500ml of red and blue dyes in separate plastic jugs. Set aside.

3   Referring to *Stage 3 - Setting Up Your Equipment,* set out 9 large plastic cups in a plastic tray and line each cup with a plastic bag.

4   Referring to *Stage 4 - Immersing Your Fabric in the Dye,* measure the dyes into each of the 9 cups. Wring out and immerse one piece of fabric in each cup. Then stack and cure the bags of dyed fabric for at least 3 hours.

5   Referring to *Stage 5 - Finishing Off,* rinse and scour your fabric. Then trim and iron to prepare your fabric for use.

2 tbsp (30ml) Blue
2 tbsp (30ml) Red

2 tbsp, 2 tsp(40ml) Blue
1 tbsp,1tsp (20ml) Red

3 tbsp, 1tsp (50ml) Blue
2 tsp (10ml) Red

3 tbsp, 2 ½ tsp (57.5ml) Blue
½ tsp (2.5ml) Red

4 Tbsp (60ml) Blue

1 tbsp, 1 tsp (20ml) Blue
2 tbsp,2tsp (40ml) Red

2 tsp(10ml) Blue
3 tbsp,1tsp (50ml) Red

½ tsp(2.5ml) Blue
3 tbsp, 2 ½ tsp (57.5ml) Red

4 Tbsp (60ml) Red

Blue to Red Two-colour Dye Run with 7 Intermediate Colour Steps

Further Two-Colour Dye Runs

For Red to Yellow and Yellow to Blue dye runs, the process is exactly the same as shown above.

Two-Colour Dye Runs in Alternative Colour Wheels

Once you've got the hang of the two-colour process, why stop at the basic primaries? You can try this process using not just primary colours but any two colours you can think of.

Two-Colour Dye Runs Using Complementary Colours

You could try dyeing a run between two complementary colours such as yellow and purple, red and green and blue and orange. When you do this you will reveal the rich neutral shades that nestle in between these striking shades.

Getting More From Each Dye Session

Up until now, I've been showing how to dye relatively small quantities of fabric. If it's for your personal use that may be all you want. But, if you want to produce enough to either sell to your friends, sewing class clients or in your online shops, you're probably going to want to produce much more from each dye session.

Expanding Your Output

In this section I am going to show you how, by doubling the quantity of dye and increasing the length of your dyeing session from one to two days, you can produce ten times the number of fat quarters you would normally produce from a standard 12-step dyeing session and no two will be the same.

Getting More Value

The secret of this huge increase in production is getting more values from each colour. Value is the depth of shade of a particular colour i.e. how light or dark it is. Changing the value of your dyed fabric from its full intensity to increasingly lighter values (each step is called a *gradation*) is achieved by two methods:

• Adding an extra piece of fabric to each plastic bag

• Diluting the dyes with an equal amount of water for each gradation.

You can, of course make as many or as few gradations as you wish of each colour. I usually do ten of each colour making two pieces in each of five bags.

Even though we will be putting two pieces of fabric in each plastic bag, they will not come out the same depth of colour. The first piece to go in will absorb the majority of the dye molecules but there will still be plenty floating around. These will be mostly be absorbed by the second piece. So even though you have two pieces in the same bag, one will be lighter than the other.

Tablecloth Using Three Gradations of Each Colour

Doubling Up the Dye

As you are going to be putting two pieces of fabric in each bag you are going to need double the amount of dye that you would normally use for each step of the 12-step colour wheel.

If you look back at *The 12-Step "Pure" Colour Wheel*, you will see that the quantity of dye required for each step adds up to 4 tablespoons, or 60ml. So if this is doubled you will need 8 tablespoons or 120ml for each step.

Notes:
When we start using larger quantities like this, it is much easier to measure the diluted dye in a small jug than by tablespoons.

When producing such large quantities of fabric, it is advisable to work with just one colour at a time, soaking the fabric, measuring the dye and immersing and setting the fabric to cure.

Dyeing Five (or Ten) Gradations of a Colour

To produce five different values of one of the colours of your 12-step colour wheel, proceed as follows:

Note:
If you are planning to dye five different gradations, and 10 pieces, for each step of the 12-step colour wheel, you will need to mix 1000ml (32oz or 4 cups) of each of the red blue and yellow dyes using the ratio of dye powder to water give in *The 12-Step "Pure" Colour Wheel*.

1   Set out 10, plastic-bag lined cups.

2   Measure out double the amount of dye required, for the colour you are dyeing, into a small measuring jug. It should measure 120ml (4 floz or ½ cup).

3   Pour the dye into the first cup.

Note:
If you are dyeing a colour that is made up of two different dyes, red and blue or blue and yellow, remember that you will need to double the quantities of each dye colour.

4   Place one piece of fabric into the cup, and massage the dye through it as detailed in *Stage 4 - Immersing Your Fabric* in the Dye. Repeat with the second piece, forcing the remaining dye through the fabric.

5   Seal the bag and set aside.

6   Pour another 120ml of dye into the second cup and add 120ml of lukewarm water. Stir.

7   Pour half of this mixture (120ml) into the third cup and place two pieces of fabric into it as before.

8   Add 120ml of lukewarm water to the remaining 120ml dye in the jug and stir.

9   Pour half of this mixture (120ml) into the fourth cup and place two pieces of fabric into it as before.

10 Add 120ml of lukewarm water to the remaining 120ml dye in the jug and stir.

11 Pour half of this mixture (120ml) into the fifth cup and place two pieces of fabric into it as before.

12 You can either discard the remaining diluted dye or pour it into another cup and add two more pieces of fabric!

"Tie-Dyeing" Made Easy

Remember the tie-dyeing lessons at school? All that tying of knots and twanging of elastic bands. The age it took to untie or cut them all of without cutting holes in the fabric. And then, of course, the inevitable splodgy hippie T-shirt. We all had one – and some of us – ahem – are still wearing them.

A New Way to "Tie-Dye"

Now there is an easier way to get fab, groovy designs without so much winding and tying. It's probably not that new but still easier.

This method relies more on careful folding, stuffing into jars and pouring dye over than the original method.

The results - this of course depends on which colours you decided to use - can be subtle, evocative and provide the perfect foil for adding photographs or text.

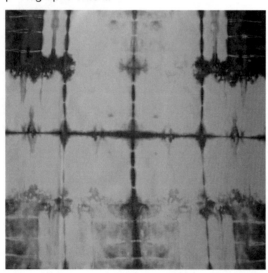

How To "Tie-Dye" Your Fabric

For this exercise you will need a couple of small jam jars, some string or elastic bands, as many fat quarters of pre-soaked fabric (dried) as you want to dye and your dye mix.

The proportion of dye powder to water is exactly the same as that for *The 12-Step "Pure" Colour Wheel*.

Squared Pattern

I really liked this pattern as, being very keen on photos printed onto fabric, I could see the possibility of appliquéing black and white family photos into the pale squares.

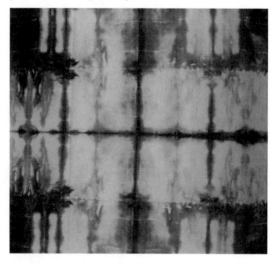

To achieve this pattern:

1   Take a fat quarter of pre-soaked, dry cotton and keep folding it in half until you are left with a 4"square (approximately).

2   Roll it up into a cigar shape and secure with a couple of elastic bands.

3   Push right down into the jar.

4   Pour over enough dye mix to cover.

5   Put the jar lid on or cover the top with cling film.

6   Cure for the time necessary for your dye colour.

7   Rinse, wash, trim and iron.

Accordion Pattern

I thought this particular pattern would be great for family trees, with all the spaces for names, or for notebook covers. You could print out lots of names or meaningful sayings onto fabric and then appliqué them into the spaces.

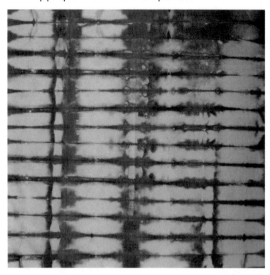

The grey one below has a much more decorative look to it and reminded me of all those wrought-iron chapels you see in churches surrounding the tombs of long-dead saints.

To achieve this pattern:

1   Take a fat quarter of pre-soaked, dry cotton and fold in accordion pleats all the way across the fabric.

2   Fold both ends in so they meet in the middle, then fold the strip in half again.

3   Secure with a couple of elastic bands.

4   Push right down into the jar.

5   Pour over enough dye mix to cover.

6   Put the jar lid on or cover the top with cling film.

7   Cure for the time necessary for your dye colour.

8   Rinse, wash, trim and iron.

Diagonal Accordion Pattern

This is basically the same as the previous pattern except the pleats are folded starting at one corner instead of from one long edge. But it has a dramatically different look and makes me think of spinal X-rays.

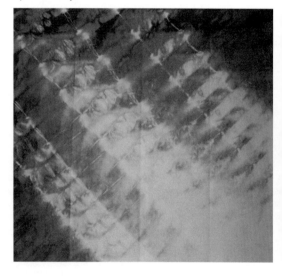

Experiment!

These are just a few ideas for achieving pattern in dyed fabric but I'm sure there are many more. Don't be afraid to experiment. If you don't like the finished result you can always over-dye it or even fold it up in a different way and dye it in another colour.

Dyeing Larger Pieces of Fabric

It is great fun dyeing fat quarters in loads of different colours. But once you have dyed, cut and pieced your quilt, what do you back it with?

Why Larger Pieces?

I have lost count of the number of times my sewing workshops customers, after spending a fortune in fabric and time constructing a double quilt or a large throw said, "I've got a polycotton sheet at home, I'll use that. It doesn't matter about the back, nobody will see that!"

But that, as I was at pains to convince the most ardent of sheet-backers, is just not true. Quilts are turned back to show the reverse. Throws are thrown and snuggled and cuddled and both sides are seen. I think that if you've spent all that time on a project you owe it to yourself – and the recipient of your project – to finish it properly by adding a back that complements the front.

If you've made a large project from your hand-dyed fabrics and intend to back it with the same, you will need to dye larger pieces.

Dyeing Large

Obviously, it's not practical to heave 2 metres of dripping wet fabric into a plastic bag and massage the dye through it.

There are two ways to produce large dyed pieces without too much effort and the one that you use will depend on the effect you want.

If you are happy to have a hand-dyed piece of fabric that is the colour you want but has a very even coverage, i.e. it doesn't have all the blotches and patterning that those dyed in plastic bags do, then it is best to dye it in your washing machine.

If you want a piece that has lots of patterning and irregularities in the dyeing – probably more than the fat quarters – then it is best to dye it in a bucket.

Dyeing in Your Washing Machine

Some people are horrified when I tell them that I dye fabrics in my washing machine, especially when two of my daughters are chefs and I wash their whites in the same machine. But I have never had a problem with dyes affecting my household washing as, during the dyeing process, the fabric, and machine are rinsed so thoroughly that there is little risk of any residue remaining.

Strong Even Colours Dyed in a Washing Machine

If you would like to try dyeing larger pieces in your washing machine, here is the process I use.

You will need:

- The piece of fabric you want to dye. 4m is the maximum I would attempt in a standard washing machine. You will need to weigh your fabric and for each 100g you will need:
  - 0.2-1g of dye powder for pale shades
  - 2-3g of dye powder for medium shades
  - 6.8g of dye powder for strong shades i.e. black or navy
- Plastic measuring jug
- 500g (1lb) of common salt
- 35g (2 heaped tbsp) Soda ash or washing soda

- Timer

Note
When dying in a washing machine, the quantities of salt and soda ash are always the same but the weight of dye required is dependent on the weight of the dry fabric.

Then proceed as follows:

1 Check that your fabric is clean and has not been dressed with any sizing or starch. If unsure, wash the fabric at 60°C putting ½ tsp of Synthrapol in the detergent drawer for each metre.

2 Calculate the dye you will need and place in the measuring jug.

3 Add a little water and mix to a smooth paste. Make up to 500ml (scant pint or 2 cups). Stir thoroughly.

4 Place the 500g of salt in the washing machine drum and then pour in the dye solution.

5 Add the fabric to the washing machine.

Note:
Procion dyes work best, in an automatic washing machine, at 40-50°C. Ensure that the machine is not on a pre-wash programme or the dye will drain away before the fixative (soda ash) has been added.

6 Set the machine to a 40°C or 50°C programme.

7 Set a timer for 15 minutes and start the machine.

8 Place the soda ash or washing soda in the jug and add 1 litre (2 pints of 4 cups) of warm water.

9 When the 15 minutes is up, pour the soda ash into the main powder drawer while the machine is running.

10 When the programme is finished, dry and iron your fabric.

Dyeing in a Bucket

If you want your large piece of fabric to have a similar mottled or patterned effect as your smaller fat quarters, it is better to dye it in a bucket.

I would recommend that you don't try and dye more than 2 metres of fabric using this method as it would be very difficult to turn anything larger around in the dye solution.

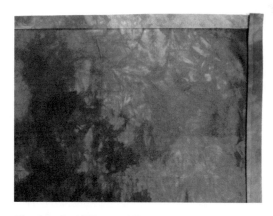

The Mottled Effects of Dyeing in a Bucket

To dye fabric in a bucket, you will need to weigh your fabric and calculate the amount of dye needed as in the washing machine instructions.

Then proceed as follows:

1 Pre-soak your fabric as shown in Pre-Soaking Your Fabric.

2 Place the dye powder in a measuring jug.

3 Add a little water and mix to a smooth paste. Make up to 500ml (scant pint or 2 cups). Stir thoroughly, then make up to 1000ml (2 pints or 4 cups).

4 Pour the dye into a clean bucket and then add another litre of warm water. Stir thoroughly.

5 Wearing rubber gloves, add the fabric to the bucket, turning it around in the liquid until there are no white patches left. Keep squeezing the dye through the fabric for several minutes.

6 Cover the bucket with cling film or a lid and leave in a warm place to cure for 3 – 24 hours depending on the colour.

7 When the curing time is up, drain away as much of the dye liquid as possible then tip the remaining liquid and fabric into the washing machine.

8 Set the machine to rinse and spin (this may be two separate programmes on some machines).

9 Add ½ tsp of Synthrapol per metre to the washing machine main powder drawer and run a standard 40C programme.

10 Dry and iron your fabric as usual.

Part 5: Projects to Dye For

Some sewing practice for your new found dyeing skills.

 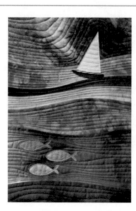  

Project – Chevron Shopper

This interesting bag has a geometric pattern that will need careful piecing to get the full effect. I've made it in bright colours but colours from any of the colour wheels given in this book will look good.

You Will Need

- **4 x fat quarters of main colour**
- **1 x fat quarter of contrast chevron colour**
- **Scrap of contrast fabric for triangle**
- **½ m of cotton batting**
- **Toning polyester thread**
- **Toning embroidery thread**

Cut Out Your Pieces

Iron your fabrics using a hot steam iron and then cut out your pattern pieces and stack in piles for easy piecing.

From the main fabric cut out:

- 3 x rectangles 15" x 13½" for bag back and lining
- 1 x strip 3" x 13½" for front top
- 5 x strips 20" x 2" for chevrons
- 2 x strips 20" x 4 for handles
- 2 x strips 4½" x 4" for handles

From the contrast chevron fabric, cut out:

- 5 x strips 20" x 2" for chevrons

From the contrast triangle fabric, cut out:

- 1 x 6" square cut diagonally in half to make 2 triangles

Machine Setup

All seam allowances are ¼" (1cm) unless stated otherwise.

A standard zigzag foot is used throughout unless otherwise stated.

To Make Your Bag

Make the Front Panel

1   Take one of the triangles and the 2" wide strips in the main and contrast colours and, using a scant ¼" seam allowance, stitch together referring to the following diagram and the project photo.

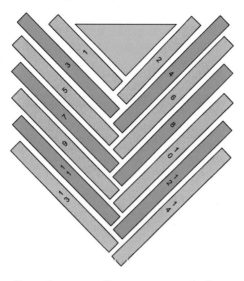

2   Press the seam allowances towards the triangle.

3   Using the top edge of the triangle as the top edge of your front pieced panel, trim the front panel to a rectangle measuring 13½" wide x 12½" deep. The bottom corners of the rectangle should touch the outer edges of strips 13 and 14.

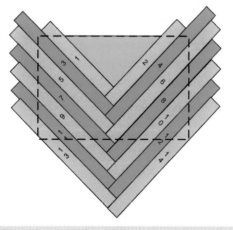

Note:
Use the trimmings to make a coin purse to match your bag!

4   Take the 3" x 13½" strip in the main colour and pin it, right sides together, along the top of the bag front. Stitch.

5   Press the seam open.

6   Cut a piece of batting ½" larger all round than the bag pieced front. Place the batting on the ironing board and the pieced rectangle on top. Press.

7   Secure the two layers with a few quilters' safety pins.

8   Thread the top of your machine with a toning embroidery thread and the bobbin with toning polyester.

9   Set your stitch length for 3mm and make neat lines of stitching down each side of each diagonal strip. Line up the edge of your presser foot with the seam lines to help you to keep the stitching straight.

Assemble Bag Back

10   Add the wadding to the back panel as described for the front and quilt as desired. Either equally spaced vertical lines or a pattern similar to the piecing of the front panel would be suitable.

Make the Handles

11   Join handle sections to form 2 x pieces 24" x 3". Press seams open.

12   From the remaining wadding, cut two strips 24" x 1".

13   Lay one of the 1" strips of wadding centrally down one of the handle pieces.

14   Turn in one long edge to the centre of the wadding strip and press.

15   Fold in ¼" of the other long edge and press. Fold again so the fold covers the raw edge.

16   Press and pin in place.

17   Stitch six equally spaced lines of stitching down the length of the handle making sure the centre one is holding the fold in place over the raw edge.

18   On the top edge of the front panel, mark a point 2½" in from each side edge.

59

19 Place the handles as shown in the diagram, lining up the outside edge of the handle with the 2" mark and making sure that the handle is not twisted and the fold will be on the inside when the handle is in use.

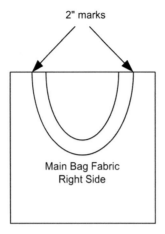

20 Repeat for the back panel and machine-tack the handles in place.

Assemble the Bag

21 Take one lining piece and place it face down on the front of the bag so the shorter edges are aligned.

22 Pin along the top edge ensuring that the raw edges of the handles are secured.

23 Stitch using a ½" seam. Press seam open.

24 Repeat with the back panel.

25 Now lay the front panel and the attached lining, on a flat surface, face up with the lining opened out.

26 Lay the back panel and attached lining on top face down so the lining is lying on top of the front panel lining. Ensure that the handles are not going to get caught in the seams.

27 Pin all the way round, leaving a gap of about 8" in the base of the lining for turning. Ensure the seams joining the lining to the bag are accurately matched up.

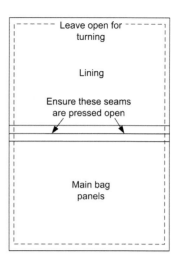

28 Now stitch all the way round using a ½" seam, leaving the 8" gap open.

29 To box the lower corners of the bag and lining sections, fold and crease the bottom between the side seams. Arrange each lower corner to form a point as shown, the side seam aligned with the pressed crease.

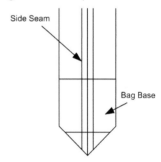

30 Measure 1" in from each point and draw a line across the point.

31 Stitch several times across the line. Do this slowly to prevent the machine jamming in the thick fabric.

32 Do not trim away excess at point.

33 Turn bag right way out, push out corners.

34 Turn in seam allowance in turning gap and stitch close to the folded edge.

35 Push lining into bag.

36 Press around top of bag ensuring seam is right on the edge.

37 For a sharper edge, stitch a line of top-stitching ¼" from the bag top.

38 For a professional finish – press thoroughly.

Project – Autumn Leaves Tablecloth

This vibrant tablecloth uses three different values of each of four colours in the flying geese panel. This is a great project for using your colour gradation experiments.

You Will Need

- **12 Fat quarters of fabric. These need to be in four different colours with one light, one medium and one dark shade in each colour.**
- **1m of 45" wide fabric for wide borders**
- **1 x backing piece 47" x 47"**
- **½m 45" wide fabric for binding**
- **Fabric scraps for appliqué images**
- **Steam-a-seam for appliqué images**
- **Template for appliqué images**
- **Sewing Machine**
- **Toning all-purpose thread**

Cut Out Your Pieces

Iron your fabrics using a hot steam iron and then cut out your pattern pieces and stack in piles for easy piecing.

- 5 x 5¼" squares in the lightest shade of each of the four colours
- 20 x 2⅞" squares in the medium shade each of the four colours
- 10 x 2½" x 8½" strips in the darkest value each of the four colours
- 4 x 32" x 8½" strips for wide borders
- 1 x backing piece 47" x 47"
- 5 x 4" strips across the width of the binding fabric

To Make Your Tablecloth

Make Your Flying Geese Squares

1 Lay one 5¼" square face up on a flat surface.

2 Place two 2⅞" squares (in the same colour range) face down on the larger square as shown below.

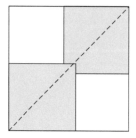

3 Draw a diagonal line through both small squares as shown.

4 Stitch on either side of the diagonal line leaving a ¼" seam allowance.

61

5 Cut along the diagonal line.

6 Press the small triangles away from the large ones.

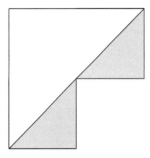

7 Place one small square face down on each of the two triangle pieces and draw a diagonal line as shown.

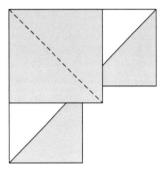

8 Stitch on either side of the diagonal line leaving a ¼" seam allowance.

9 Cut along the diagonal line.

10 Press the small triangles away from the large one forming four flying geese blocks like the one shown below.

11 Join the four blocks to form a strip as shown below.

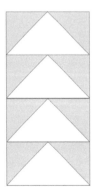

12 Trim each block to measure 4" x 8½".

13 Stitch one of the 2½" x 8½" strips (in the same colour range) to each of the long edges of the block.

14 Make all 20 blocks in the same manner.

15 Press thoroughly.

16 Trim all blocks to 8½" square.

Assemble Your Tablecloth Centre

17 Arrange 16 of the blocks into a pleasing arrangement. An example is shown below.

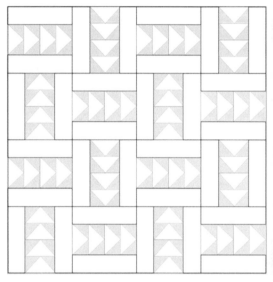

18 Stitch the blocks first into rows using a ¼" seam. Press the seam allowances in alternate directions i.e. press those in row 1 to the right, those in row 2 to the left and so on.

19 Join the rows together, interlocking the seam allowances and pinning the seams together before stitching.

20 Stitch using a ¼" seam.

21 Press these seams open.

Make Your Borders

22 Trace the appliqué shapes on the template onto the Steam-a-Seam. Group similar items together. You will need five different leaf shapes for each wide border.

23 Roughly cut out each group of shapes keeping those of the same colour together.

24 Remove one paper backing from the pieces ensuring that the glue layer remains with the remaining paper backing (the one you traced the shapes onto).

25 Finger press each group of shapes onto the appropriate colour fabric.

26 Once you are happy with the positioning of the shapes, press carefully with a medium iron.

Note:
Take care that the entire glue layer is underneath the paper backing or it will stick to the iron. I keep a spare 'glue iron' for jobs like this avoiding the need to scrape the gluey deposits of my steam iron!

27 Carefully cut out the shapes and divide them into four groups with sufficient pieces for each border in each group.

28 Iron one of the border pieces and lay it flat on the table.

29 Arrange the appliqué shapes until you are happy with the design.

30 Once you are satisfied with the design, remove the paper backings and press the pieces into place using a medium iron.

31 Set your machine for free-machine embroidery and, using appropriately coloured machine-embroidery threads, stitch pieces in place.

32 Add embroidered leaf veins and stalks.

33 Repeat for remaining border pieces

Assemble Your Tablecloth

34 Stitch one border piece to each of two opposite ends of your tablecloth.

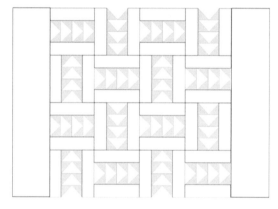

35 Take one of the remaining 8½" border pieces and attach one flying geese block to each end, ensuring that the seams line up with the joining seam lines of the first two borders.

36 Stitch the borders to the tablecloth as shown below.

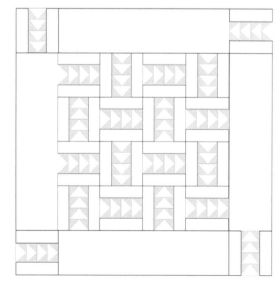

63

37 Press all border seam allowances towards borders.

38 Iron the backing fabric and lay it flat on the table.

39 Lay the tablecloth on top and carefully cut backing to the same size.

40 Join all binding strips, short ends together. Press seams open.

41 Fold binding in half lengthways and press.

42 Apply binding to two opposite ends of tablecloth, through the tablecloth and backing, raw edges together. Stitch in place.

43 Flip the binding over to the back of the cloth and press.

44 Now fold the binding over until the folded edge meets the line of stitching. Press and pin in place.

45 Apply binding to the two remaining edges, leaving 1" overhang at each end. Stitch in place.

46 Turn the 1" overhang, at each end, inwards and then fold binding as before, to form a perfect corner. Pin and stitch in place using small, neat hand stitches.

47 Quilt around each flying geese square and along each border seam using quilting thread on the top and all-purpose polyester on the bottom.

48 Give the whole tablecloth a final good steam press and hang to dry.

Project – Log Cabin Cushion with Buttoned Back

This striking cushion uses several different gradations of three colours. The back is made of panels of the three colours and fastened with wooden buttons.

You Will Need

- **3 fat quarters of full strength dyed fabric, one each in royal blue, magenta and green.**
- **Large scraps of fabric in various gradations of royal blue, magenta and green**
- **19" square of cotton batting**
- **2 x strips 1½" x 18" medium-weight fusible interfacing**

- **3 x ¾" wooden buttons (or buttons of your choice).**
- **18" cushion pad.**

Cut Out Your Pieces

Note:
Full strength dyed fabric is fabric that has been dyed with the recommended dye powder to water recipe before any colour gradations have been carried out.

Iron your fabrics using a hot steam iron and then cut out your pattern pieces and stack in piles for easy piecing.

From the full strength green fabric:

- Cut 2 x rectangles 6½" x 9" for cushion back.
- Cut several strips, of varying widths across the length of the fabric for log cabin panel.

From the full strength blue fabric:

- Cut 2 x rectangles 6½" x 9" for cushion back.
- Cut 4 x strips 3" x 20" for binding
- Cut several strips, of varying widths across the length of the fabric for log cabin panel.

From the full strength magenta fabric:

- Cut a 3" square for the cushion centre.
- Cut 2 x rectangles 6½" x 9" for cushion back.
- Cut 2 x strips 3½" x 18" for the button bands.
- Cut several strips, of varying widths across the length of the fabric for log cabin panel.

From the fabric in various gradations of the three colours:

- Cut several strips of varying widths across the length of the fabric in each colour for log cabin panel.

Machine Setup

All seam allowances are ¼" (1cm) unless stated otherwise.

A standard zigzag foot is used throughout unless otherwise stated.

To Make Your Cushion

Make Your Log Cabin Panel

1   Take your 3" square and lay one end of one of the fabric strips (cut for the log cabin panel) face down on the square.

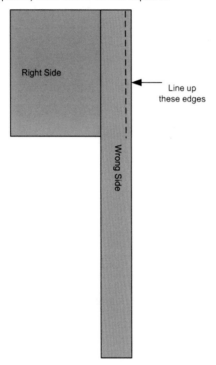

2   Using a toning thread, stitch as shown in the diagram.

3   Trim the strip off level with the bottom edge of the square, open out the strip and press the seam allowances towards the strip.

4   Take another strip and lay it face down as shown in the diagram below.

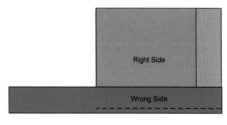

5   Stitch, trim and press as before.

6   Take another strip, this time one from the colour gradation selection and lay it face down as shown in the diagram below.

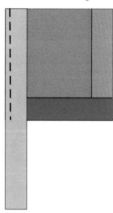

7   Stitch, trim and press as before.

8   Take another strip, one from the colour gradation selection and lay it face down as shown in the diagram below.

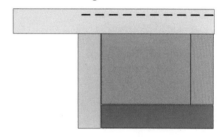

9   Stitch, trim and press as before.

10 You have now completed the first row of your log cabin panel.

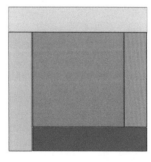

11 Continue in this manner, adding strips in a clockwise direction and keeping the darker strips on two sides of the square and the lighter ones on the other two sides, until your square measures 19" square.

Quilt Your Panel

12 You can of course quilt your front panel in any manner you choose. I quilted mine by making lines of stitching through the centre of each strip using a white embroidery thread.

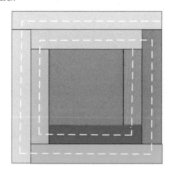

13 To quilt as shown in the diagram and photograph, set your machine to a 3mm stitch length, start at the top of the first strip you joined and continue stitching as shown.

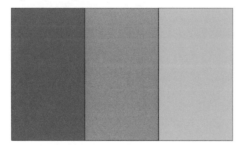

14 Trim your completed log cabin panel to an 18" square.

Make Your Cushion Back

15 Take one each of the blue, green and pink 6½" x 9" rectangles and join them together by their long sides.

16 Press the seam allowances open.

17 Repeat with the three other rectangles.

18 Take one of the 3½" x 18 strips and pin one of the long edges face down onto one of the long edges of one of the rectangle blocks. Stitch.

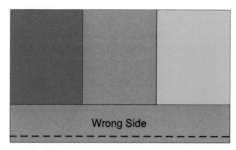

Wrong Side

19 Turn over a ¼" hem on the other long edge of the strip and press.

20 Now flip the strip over and press, then fold the strip in half towards the back of the block so the pressed and folded edge meets the line of stitching.

21 Take one of the strips of medium-weight fusible interfacing and slip it inside the folded strip, tucking the edge under the pressed ¼" hem.

22 Press the folded strip thoroughly so the interfacing adheres to the fabric.

23 Set your machine to a 3mm stitch length and work two rows of top stitching $^1/_8$" from each edge of the strip.

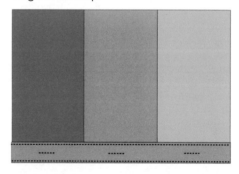

24 Set your machine for buttonholes and work three buttonholes, in the positions shown, which are ¼" longer than the diameter of your buttons.

25 Add the strip to the other half of the cushion back as before but add buttons to match the positions of the buttonholes.

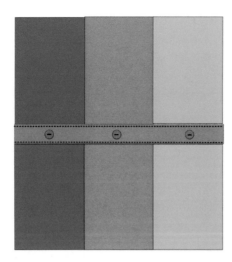

26 Trim the completed back panel to an 18" square.

Make Your Binding

27 Lay the completed back panel face down on a flat surface.

28 Lay the front log cabin panel face up on top of the back panel.

29 Pin the two panels together to prevent them slipping when you add the binding.

30 Take your four binding strips, fold them in half lengthways, and press.

31 Lay one of the binding strips onto one of the cushion panel edges, raw edges together. Stitch along the raw edge, leaving a ¼" seam allowance.

32 Flip the binding over to the back of the cushion cover and press.

33 Now fold the binding over until the folded edge meets the line of stitching. Press and pin in place.

34 Apply the other short binding strip to the opposite edge of the panel and press and pin as before.

35 Apply the longer binding strips to the two remaining edges, leaving 1" overhang at each end. Stitch in place.

36 Turn the 1" overhang, at each end, inwards and then fold binding as before, to form a

perfect corner. Pin and stitch in place using small, neat hand stitches.

37 Insert your cushion pad.

Project - Laptop Case

I made this laptop case to fit a 13" laptop but you can adjust the size to fit any size of laptop or tablet, just cut your panels 2" wider and deeper than the size of your device.

You Will Need

- **2 x fat quarters of main colour**
- **2 x fat quarter of contrast lining**
- **1 x fat quarter of binding fabric**
- **½ m of cotton batting**
- **3 ¾" diameter buttons**
- **Toning polyester thread**
- **Toning embroidery thread**

Cut Out Your Pieces

Iron your fabrics using a hot steam iron and then cut out your pattern pieces and stack in piles for easy piecing

From the main fabric cut out:

- 1 x rectangle 15" x 14" for bag back
- 1 x rectangle 15" x 10" for bag front

From the lining fabric cut out:

- 1 x rectangle 15" x 14" for bag back
- 1 x rectangle 15" x 10" for bag front

From the binding fabric cut:

- 5 x strips 17" x 3"

From the cotton batting, cut out:

- 1 x rectangle 15" x 14" for bag back
- 1 x rectangle 15" x 10" for bag front

Machine Setup

All seam allowances are ¼" (1cm) unless stated otherwise.

A standard zigzag foot is used throughout unless otherwise stated.

To Make Your Laptop Case

Make the Front Panel

1 Take the 15" x 10" rectangle of lining fabric and lay it face down on a flat surface. Lay the 15" x 10" cotton batting on top followed by the 15" x 10" main fabric.

2 Press the layers with a hot iron then add a few randomly place pins to prevent the layers slipping.

3 Thread the top of your machine with embroidery thread and the bobbin with a toning polyester thread. Set the stitch length to 3mm.

4 If you have a quilting bar, which will allow you to make evenly spaced rows of stitching without marking each row, fit it now to your presser foot.

5 Using tailor's chalk, mark a line across the panel at 45 degrees to one of the long edges of the panel. Stitch along this line and then stitch either side of the line, keeping the lines

of stitching 1½" apart, until you reach the edges of the panel.

6   Now draw a line at 90 degrees to the first and repeat the stitching as described to form a crosshatch design as shown in the project photo.

Make the Back Panel

7   Make the back panel in the same way as the front panel.

Add the Binding

8   Take your five binding strips, fold them in half lengthways, and press.

9   Lay one of the binding strips onto one of the long edges of the front panel, raw edges together. Stitch along the raw edges leaving a ¼" seam allowance. Trim the ends of the binding flush with the panel.

10 Flip the binding over to the back of the front panel and press.

11 Now fold the binding over until the folded edge meets the line of stitching. Press and pin in place. Stitch using small, neat hand stitching.

12 Lay the back panel face down on a flat surface and lay the front panel face up on top with the long raw edges lined up at the lower edge. Pin together to prevent the layers shifting.

13 Apply binding to the two sides of the case as described for the top edge of the front panel and trim the ends of the binding flush with the top and bottom edges of the case.

14 Apply the remaining binding strips to the top and bottom edges of the case, leaving 1" overhang at each end. Stitch in place.

15 Turn the 1" overhang, at each end, inwards and then fold binding as before, to form a perfect corner. Pin and stitch in place using small, neat hand stitches.

Add Your Buttons

16 Set your sewing machine for buttonholes.

Note:
As the method of stitching buttonholes varies from machine to machine, you will need to read your instruction manual to familiarise yourself with the method for your particular machine.

17 Make three evenly spaced buttonholes along the top edge of the back panel or flap, ¾" from the binding.

18 Fold over the flap and sew on the buttons to match the buttonholes.

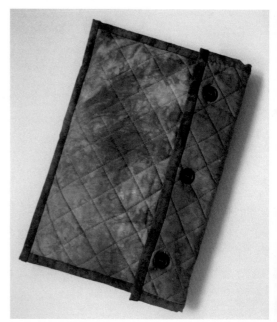

70

Project – Stripy Handbag with Yacht Appliqué

This tablecloth has a central panel of flying geese blocks which are made in 3 different values of four colours.

You Will Need

- **3 contrasting fat quarters (1 x blue, 1 x white and 1 for the lining and zip supports)**
- **Small pieces of contrasting fabric for multi-coloured handles**
- **¼ m medium weight fusible interfacing**
- **¼ m cotton wadding**
- **10" nylon dress zip in a toning colour**
- **All-purpose toning thread**
- **Rayon embroidery thread (optional)**
- **Piece of fusible web**
- **Scraps of coloured fabric for sail appliqués**

Cut Out Your Pieces

Iron your fabrics using a hot steam iron and then cut out your pattern pieces and stack in piles for easy piecing

For the bag front cut:

- 6 x asymmetrical strips 14" long x 2½" narrowing to 1½" – 3 in each of the blue and white
- 1 x 2" x 14" strip in the blue
- 2 x pieces medium weight fusible interfacing 13" x 10"
- 1 x piece wadding 13" x 10"

For the bag back:

- 1 x piece 13" x 10" in blue
- 1 x piece wadding 13 " x 10"

For the handles

- 1 x piece 6" x 3" in each of 4 colours for each handle
- 2 x strips wadding 1" x 20"

For the lining

- 2 x pieces 13" x 10"
- 2 x rectangles 4" x 10" for zip supports
- 2 x rectangles 2½" x 1½" for zip tab

To Make Your Bag

Assemble Your Bag Front

1 Take the 6 x asymmetrical strips and arrange them as shown in the diagram.

2 Stitch together using a ¼" seam (line up with the edge of your presser foot).

3 Add the 2" strip to the top of the asymmetrical block.

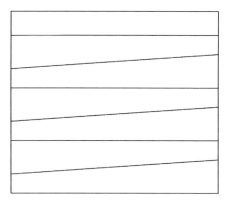

4 Press the seams open.

5 Take one of the pieces of interfacing and with the iron set to a wool setting, fuse the interfacing to the back of the pieced panel.

6 Trim the panel to 13" x 10".

7 Place one of the wadding pieces behind the pieced panel and pin in place.

Add Your Yachts

8 On the fusible web (the side with the glue sheet attached) draw a variety of different-sized triangles. I used 8 but you can vary the number or size to your taste.

9 Roughly cut out each triangle.

10 Remove the paper backing from each triangle and, using a dry iron set to the wool setting, fuse each one to a different coloured fabric scrap.

11 Carefully cut out each triangle.

12 Arrange your triangles on the bag front until you are happy with their position.

13 Remove the second paper backing and press the triangles in place.

14 If you are still happy with the arrangement, fuse the sails in place as before.

Add Your Machine Embroidery

Note:
The embroidery on the bag front can be achieved using either free-arm embroidery or a standard foot and straight stitch. The project will benefit from using rayon embroidery thread to make the design stand out.

15 Set your machine for the type of stitching you have decided on.

16 Using a variegated thread (or changing the colours as necessary) stitch around the sails overlapping the stitching onto neighbouring sails and adding a few sail outlines.

17 Change your thread to a white or pale variegated thread and add some wavy lines beneath the sails. The effect will be better if the lines are kept parallel and about ¼" apart.

Assemble Bag Back

18 Add the fusible interfacing and wadding to the back panel as described for the front and quilt as desired. Either equally spaced vertical lines or a pattern similar to the piecing of the front panel would be suitable.

Make the Handles

19 For each handle take 4 of the 6" x 3" rectangles one in each colour, and join the short ends together using a ¼" seam.

20 Press the seams open.

21 Lay one of the 1" strips of wadding centrally down one of the handle pieces.

22 Turn in one long edge to the centre of the wadding strip and press.

23 Fold in ¼" of the other long edge and press. Fold again so the fold covers the raw edge.

24 Press and pin in place.

25 Stitch six equally spaced lines of stitching down the length of the handle making sure the centre one is holding the fold in place over the raw edge.

26 Trim each handle to 20" by trimming an equal amount from each end.

27 On the top edge of the front panel, mark a point 2¾" in from each side edge.

28 Place the handles as shown in the diagram, lining up the outside edge of the handle with the mark and making sure that the handle is not twisted and the fold will be on the inside when the handle is in use.

2 3/4" marks

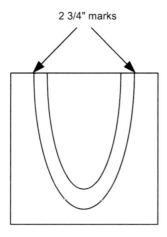

29 Repeat for the back panel and machine-tack the handles in place.

Inserting the Concealed Zip

30 Take the 2 rectangles of zip tab fabric and place them right sides together (if the fabric has a right and wrong side).

31 Using an $\frac{1}{8}$" seam allowance, stitch all the way round the rectangles, leaving 1½" opening on one of the long sides for turning.

32 Clip the corners, turn and press.

33 Take the permanently closed end of the zip, fold the zip tab in half lengthways and slip it over the end of the zip effectively covering the crimped end.

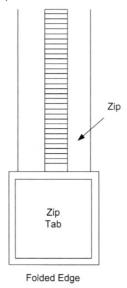

Zip

Zip
Tab

Folded Edge

34 Stitch round the zip tab, as shown in the diagram) securing the end of the zip inside

35 Now take one of the 4" x 10" rectangles and turn in each of the short edges by ½". Press.

36 Now fold the rectangle in half lengthways and press.

37 Open the rectangle out and turn in one of the long edges to meet the centre fold. Press.

38 Repeat with the other long edge.

39 Refold the rectangle along the centre fold and press again.

40 Repeat with second rectangle.

41 Slide one of the zip supports onto one side of the zip ensuring the raw (opening end) edge is tucked in. Pin securely.

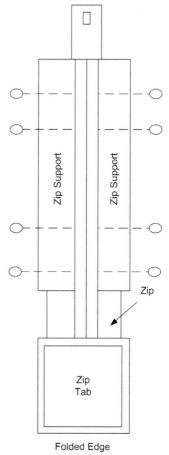

Zip Support

Zip Support

Zip

Zip
Tab

Folded Edge

42 Repeat with other support.

43 Using a zipper foot, stitch along the edge of each support close to the zip teeth.

44 After stitching ensure that the zip opens and closes smoothly.

45 Now take one of the lining panels and lay it face up on a flat surface.

46 Mark the top centre of the lining panel and the centre of each zip support with tailor's chalk

47 Place the zip as shown in the diagram, lining up the centre point of the zip support with the centre point of the lining panel and positioning the zip assembly 1¼" from the top edge of the lining.

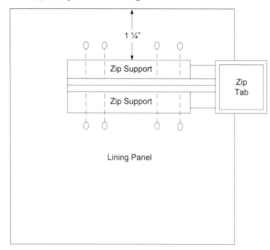

48 Using a standard presser foot and a 2.5mm straight stitch, stitch along the top of the zip support as shown in the diagram.

49 Take the second lining panel and lay face up on a flat surface.

50 Pick up the lining panel, which has the zip attached, by the zip support which is not stitched down, so the zip is facing you.

51 Hold each end of this support, one end in each hand and place it onto the second lining panel, in the same position as you placed the first side.

52 Pin and stitch as before, opening the zip to make it easier.

Note
It is important throughout the following stages to ensure that the zip is not twisted by opening and closing it periodically.

53 Place the front bag panel, with the handles attached, face up on a flat surface. Make sure the handles are laying flat on the bag front.

54 Now take the zip with the lining panels attached, picking the whole thing up by the top edge of one of the lining panels, one side in each hand, so the wrong side of the panel is facing towards you and the zip is facing away from you.

55 Lay this top edge along the top edge of the bag front so the raw edges are together.

56 Pin securely and stitch using a ¼" seam allowance.

57 Now flip the zip and lining panels over exposing the front panel.

58 Place the back bag panel, with the handles attached; face up on a flat surface. Make sure the handles are laying flat on the bag back.

59 Pick up the zip and lining piece by the top edge of the second lining panel (the one you have not yet stitched) holding one side in each hand and lay it down along the top of the right side of the back panel, raw edges together.

60 Pin securely and stitch using a ¼" seam.

61 Press both the top edge seams open.

62 Now lay the bag down on a flat surface so the bag back and front panels (right sides) are facing each other and the back and front lining panels (right sides) are also facing each other.

63 Make sure the zip is open and is not twisted.

64 Pin the raw edges together all round the bag main panel and lining, leaving an 8" gap in the bottom of the lining for turning.

65 Ensure that the top edge seams are pressed and pinned open.

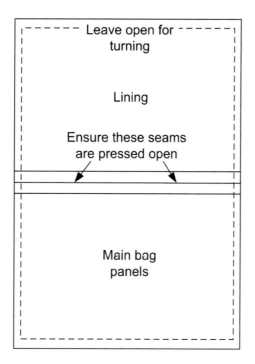

Leave open for turning

Lining

Ensure these seams are pressed open

Main bag panels

Boxing the Corners

66 To box the lower corners of the bag and lining sections, fold and crease the bottom between the side seams. Arrange each lower corner to form a point as shown, the side seam aligned with the bottom seam.

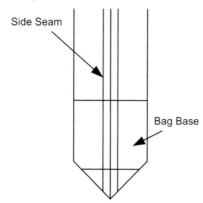

Side Seam

Bag Base

67 Measure 1" in from each point and draw a line across the point.

68 Stitch several times across the line. Do this slowly to prevent the machine jamming in the thick fabric.

Note:
Start sewing 1" in from the edge of this seam, reverse back to start (ensuring that the presser foot does not 'tip' off the edge of the fabric) then continue forward.

69 Do not trim away excess at point.

70 Using a tailor's ham or rolled-up towel, and a steam iron, press open the side seams and the seams at the top outside edges of the bag. This will make it much easier to achieve a smooth edge when turned the right way out.

71 Turn bag right way out, push out corners.

72 Turn in seam allowance in turning gap and machine-stitch close to the folded edge.

73 Push lining into bag.

74 Press around top of bag ensuring seam is right on the edge.

75 Stitch a line of top-stitching ¼" from the bag top.

76 For a professional finish – press thoroughly paying particular attention to steaming the side seams, using a ham or towel, and allowing them to cool before removing from ironing board and hanging up immediately.

Note:
Do not apply heat to the rayon embroidery stitching as it may melt and the design become distorted.

75

Part 6: What Next?

Here are some other books and inspirations you might like to look at.

 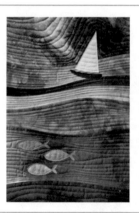  

More from Time4me Workshops

You can find more tips, techniques, books and videos on my website.

Time4me-Workshops Website

The aim of my website is to promote traditional crafts by passing on knowledge, skills and experience to those who would like to learn about, or perhaps already enjoy, sewing.

In these pages you will find practical advice that will make your sewing projects easier and more enjoyable. You'll find advice on choosing and using wadding, getting started in dressmaking and top tips on appliqué.

Why not take a look at my videos on how to use men's shirts to make a traditional quilt? Or if cushion making is more your thing, there are a series of six videos showing you all you need to know.

To find out more, visit Margo Price's website at:

time4me-workshops.co.uk

How to Make a Living from Crafts

Using the craft of sewing as an example, this book will also provide essential reading for other craftsmen such as musicians, photographers, jewellery makers, card makers, knitters, woodworkers, gardeners, watercolour painters, clay modellers, mosaic artists, and many more.

This online e-book (soon also to be available in other formats) is suited to intermediate and advanced crafters who are producing work good enough to sell or who may be selling their wares already but are struggling to make a living. It also explains the benefits of branching out and teaching your skill to others and shows you how to set up and run your workshops.

To purchase this book, or find out more, visit Margo Price's website at:

time4me-workshops.co.uk

Or visit the Kindle Store at www.amazon.co.uk or www.amazon.com

How to Sew With Confidence

Do you want to make the designs you see in sewing magazines or on the web? Has your sewing machine been lurking in the under stairs cupboard since you bought it? Do you lack the confidence to take control of your sewing machine?

This book provides the perfect jargon-free starter guide for those who would love to master their sewing machine. With a collection of simple, but stylish, sewing projects and a detailed reference section of basic techniques, this book guides you, step-by-step, through the basics of machine sewing.

This online e-book (soon also to be available in other formats) is suited to beginners and those who want to be more confident in their sewing.

To purchase this book, or find out more, visit Margo Price's website at:

time4me-workshops.co.uk

Or visit the Kindle Store at www.amazon.co.uk or www.amazon.com

How to Get Started in Free-Machine Embroidery

Do you want to be more creative with your sewing? Do you want to learn how to get more from your sewing machine? Do you lack the confidence to get started in machine embroidery?

This book provides the ideal jargon-free beginners guide for those who want to explore free-machine embroidery. With a collection of creative sewing projects and individual sections for mastering basic techniques, this book guides you, step-by-step, through the basics of free-machine embroidery.

In this book, Margo Price shares her tried-and-tested techniques and sewing projects, perfected over ten-year's experience of running her own sewing business "Time4me Workshops". The practical ideas presented in this book will provide essential reading for anyone wanting an easy-to-understand introduction to the fascinating world of free-machine embroidery.

To purchase this book, or find out more, visit Margo Price's website at:

time4me-workshops.co.uk

Or visit the Kindle Store at www.amazon.co.uk or www.amazon.com

Please Leave a Review

If you've enjoyed this book, or any of my other books, please go to the book page on the Amazon Kindle Store and leave me a review.